Practical Hand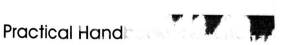

GARDEN ARCHAEOLOGY

Chris Currie

2005
Council for British Archaeology

First published in 2005 for the Council for British Archaeology
St Mary's House, 66 Bootham, York YO30 7BZ

Copyright © 2005 Author and Council for British Archaeology

British Library Cataloguing in Publication Data

A catalogue card for this book is available from the British Library

ISBN 1-902771-48-6

Typeset by M C Bishop at The Armatura Press
Printing by Pennine Printing Services

Front Cover: The Conservatory at The Grange, Northington (Hants)

Contents

Acknowledgements

The author would like to thank all those who contributed to this work, not only by their input to the volume itself (Martin Locock, Robin Turner and Iain Soden), but those who worked on the author's numerous studies mentioned herein. They include Dan Hicks, Stephanie Pinter-Bellows, Stephen Burrow, Heidi Taylor, Mark O'Brien, Andrew and Matthew Reynolds, Paul Chandler, Penny Hasler, Tim Allen, Rob Atkins, Mark Loft, Trevor Steptoe, John Hutchinson, Marion White, Neil FitzPatrick, Derek Fox, and Mark Stewart. Amongst the specialists who have worked on the author's projects were Professor Frank Chambers (pollen & soils), Stephen Gray (soils), Maria Barlow (ceramic conservation), Peter Barker of Stratascan (geophysics), Elizabeth Person and Clare de Rouffignac (Environmental Science). Special mention should be made of Clare de Rouffignac, who originally persuaded the author of the need to rethink previous opinions on sampling for seed in gardens, and for actively encouraging the team to come up with the results.

Martin Locock's assistance at Castle Bromwich and on many subsequent projects has been invaluable, as have been his contributions to this book. In more recent years many of the author's projects have been undertaken with the assistance of Dr Neil Rushton. Both Martin and Neil are largely responsible for keeping the author on the straight and narrow and for tempering his more outrageous personality defects. The author is also grateful to Iain Soden of Northampton Archaeology for providing illustrations of work by himself and his own unit, and contributing the text of one of the case studies. Robin Turner of the National Trust for Scotland is warmly thanked for stepping in at short notice to provide a case study for Scotland.

The following also made significant contributions to the thinking within this volume, even if they never realised I was paying attention: Dr Keith Goodway, Ann Kendrick, Gordon Ewart, John Phibbs, Philip Claris, David Standing, Ken Whittaker, John Hemmingway, the late Charles Munday, Sally Hocking, Sybil Wade, Gilly Drummond, Graham Gammin, David and Caroline Thackray, Cathy and Colin White, Dirk Scholtz, Katarina Frost, Ada Segre, Jeffrey Haworth, Colin Platt, John Kenyon, and Bill Klemperer

On the publication side Jane Thorniley-Walker was responsible for suggesting the project to the author and for guiding him through the many stages to final publication. The ever-knowledgeable James Bond reviewed the work and made innumerable helpful suggestions. Robert Bell provided illustrations of his sites and commented on my interpretation of his work.

List of figures

Chris Currie

Chris Currie died suddenly whilst the proofs of this handbook were in their final preparatory stages. Chris had been at the forefront of research into garden archaeology since the late 1980s and was keen for the results of his work to reach a wider audience in the synthesised format of a CBA handbook. It is a great tragedy that he will not see the publication in its final form, but it will stand as a lasting testament to Chris's innovative archaeological outlook, and will hopefully inspire a new generation of archaeologists to investigate the archaeology of British gardens.

Chris first became involved with garden archaeology in 1989 when he was appointed as a Leverhulme Research Fellow to test the application of archaeological methods to practical fieldwork on historic gardens, based at Castle Bromwich Hall, West Midlands. This led to the founding of the Gardens Archaeology Project, which amongst its projects carried out an important nine-year series of research excavations at Dartington Hall, Devon, and a long term project excavating and surveying the landscaped gardens at Bushy Park, Greater London. Over the past eleven years I have worked on many of the projects described in this handbook and, thanks to Chris, have gained an appreciation of the development of historic gardens in Britain. But there are very few archaeologists in the country who have the depth of specialist knowledge to have written a handbook such as this, and Chris was one of them. With garden restorations likely to continue in popularity over the next decades, this work sets a benchmark of archaeological professionalism that should ensure garden archaeology will always remain an essential concomitant to any restoration or development project. This will be one of Chris's most enduring legacies.

Neil Rushton

SECTION 1: INTRODUCTION

Chapter 1: The development of garden archaeology

The restoration of historic gardens has become an increasingly active area of heritage management over the last 25 years.[1] A catalyst to this process in the UK was the destruction caused by severe storms in October 1987, where large numbers of mature trees within gardens and designed landscapes were uprooted. In many cases, this was seen as an opportunity to replant in an older style, rather than to follow patterns derived from more recent changes. This gave many heritage organisations the opportunity to research previous planting schemes, and to reinstate them as a more appropriate setting contemporary with the surrounding buildings.

Although archaeology had been used in the past to obtain plans for the restoration of historic gardens (*cf* Kirby Hall, Northamptonshire, UK in the 1930s), the majority of efforts before 1987 were based on archival sources. Contemporary views, such as drawings, paintings, and plans proved to be the most popular sources used as the basis for restoration. An example of restoration at Claremont, Surrey, undertaken from 1975 onwards, has since been criticised by Nail (1997, 6) for not undertaking archaeological survey prior to the restoration of the amphitheatre there. A rare exception to this pattern was Cunliffe's work (1971)

Figure 1: Kirby Hall, Northants: Study of the 1930s' parterre *before excavations in the early 1990s revealed that previous excavation had destroyed most of the evidence for earlier designs. This is a firm warning against the use of total excavation of garden sites during restoration.*

1

at Fishbourne Roman Palace in 1962, where substantial remains of gardens were recovered solely by archaeology.

More recently it has been recognised that literal interpretation of pictorial sources can be dangerous. Drawings and paintings can contain inaccuracies. Some are not a true depiction of the garden, but a proposal or an idealisation of how the draughtsman or owner would like to see it.

Historic gardens are a unique type of archaeological site, principally because they continue to evolve. There are living components, such as trees and other plants integral to the design, which are constantly growing, altering shape and dying. Unlike an inanimate historic building, gardens are difficult to 'fossilise' into museum pieces. Despite these challenges, the rewards of garden restoration have become increasingly recognised by the heritage industry in recent years.

It has become increasingly popular to incorporate archaeology into garden restoration or rejuvenation schemes, but the implications of its use have not always been fully appreciated. A number of problems have been outlined in earlier papers by Currie (1992) and Currie and Locock (1992). Between 1989 and 1992 research funded by the Leverhulme Trust into the application of archaeological methods to historic gardens produced results that have helped towards a re-appraisal of current practice. One of the most important conclusions drawn from this was that the old style of archaeology in gardens, which was based on plan recovery, fails to realise the true potential of the resource. The use of techniques such as soil analysis and botanical sampling, thought as recently as 1991 to be often impractical in garden environments (Murphy & Scaife 1991, 85), has now been shown to offer greater scope than previously expected (Currie 1990b, 1992, 1995a; Currie & Locock 1991a).

Although it took a natural disaster to prompt interest in garden archaeology in the UK, the archaeology of the more recent past has been part of the mainstream of North American archaeological practice for much longer. Garden archaeology has been a major part of this, particularly since the encouraging results obtained by the Colonial Williamsburg Project from the 1960s (Hume 1974). Since then the Dumbarton Oaks School in the USA has continued to promote garden archaeology (Malek & Conan forthcoming), both in its invasive excavation form and in that of non-invasive survey, often involving analytical techniques based on interpretation of historic landscapes. The latter has seen a parallel growth in interest in the UK, where organisations such as Land Use Consultants and De Bois (John Phibbs) have been active since at least the early 1980s, often working in conjunction with archaeologists. Many modern landscape architect consultancies now profess an expertise in the interpretation of historic designed landscape, although genuine experience in this field is often restricted to specific individuals.

The earliest work in the UK to coin the term 'garden archaeology' was Christopher Taylor's contribution to the Shire Archaeology series (1983). Although a pioneering study, this work largely restricted itself to discussing the interpretation of earthworks, and did not pretend to cover excavation archaeology. Taylor's work was based on a programme of surveys that had been carried out by the Royal Commission on the Historical Monuments of England (RCHME) over the previous 20 years or so (RCHME 1968, 1972, 1975–82). These surveys have set the bench mark for such work, and were instrumental in providing a corpus of material that would inspire others to appreciate the scope for research of garden remains within the historic landscape, both for further survey (Brown 1991) as well as excavation. Other pioneering work

2

Figure 2: Castle Bromwich Hall, West Midlands: the gardeners told the author not to bother, the garden had been 'double-dug' recently. Despite meeting with persistent pessimism in the early days of garden archaeology in the UK, archaeologists managed to undercover this 19th-century parterre design less than 150mm below the surface. The beds had been laid out in compacted gravel hollows, thus helping to preserve them.

worthy of mention includes Beresford and St Joseph's (1958, 68–9) identification of garden earthworks at Holdenby and Harrington in Northamptonshire using aerial photography, and Aston's survey of garden earthworks at Hardington and Low Ham in Somerset (Aston 1978).

The main phase of recent excavations started in Scotland, with Hynd and Ewart's (1983) work at Aberdour Castle in Scotland. Public attention in England was attracted by a number of projects with their origins in the early 1980s. Painshill in Surrey used the government-sponsored Manpower Services Scheme to sponsor excavation work there in the early 1980s. This was followed by another Manpower Services Scheme at Castle Bromwich Hall, West Midlands. The early work here was summarised by the present authors (Locock & Currie 1991), and later supplemented by research excavations funded by the Leverhulme Trust between 1989 and 1992 (Currie 1990; Currie and Locock 1993a, 1993b). In the meantime, the restoration of a Georgian town garden at Bath in 1986 was preceded by excavations by Robert Bell (1990). It was the encouraging results from early sites such as these that inspired many others to follow suit.

Between 1985 and 1989 a number of projects were begun, although many of these have yet to be fully reported. One of the principal characteristics of these early projects was the aim of a specific 'single-period' restoration. Here sites were restored, as near as possible, to their condition at a single date in the past. Many of these encountered

3

Figure 3: Château de la Roche Courbon, Poitou Charentes, France. A 19th-century restoration of the French-style landscape. How much is fanciful without the benefit of archaeology is a moot point? (Copyright Iain Soden)

problems in that the date chosen was often that for which the archaeology was the least well preserved. Of these projects of the later 1980s, the two most notable published examples were Bell's work at Painswick, Gloucestershire, and an English Heritage project at Kirby Hall, Northamptonshire (Bell 1993, Dix *et al* 1995).

Although the Painswick project was largely successful in achieving its single period aim other projects were not so fortunate. At Kirby Hall the evidence for the period selected had disappeared, and the site was eventually restored to a contemporary plan for Longleat House, Wiltshire. Castle Bromwich had to adjust its projected date of 1730 to keep in touch with new discoveries that much of the garden had been built after that date. At Tredegar House, Newport (formerly Monmouthshire), a formal garden excavated between 1989 and 1990, the results differed from those originally envisaged. The resulting restoration, although essentially accurate, has disappointed many garden historians by being too spartan, with less plant interest than they would have hoped.

More recently the single period approach has been questioned as a desirable aim (Currie 1992, 183–84; Currie & Scholz 1996). Many gardens proposing restoration now opt for a broader time span, or choose to restore different parts of the garden to that period most appropriate to the existing remains.

The 1990s continued to see much interest in the use of archaeology in gardens. Many of these projects took advantage of the results of the Leverhulme research project emanating from Castle Bromwich Hall to incorporate soil analysis and environmental sampling. Gordon Ewart's work at Tredegar House, was the earliest project to do this, commissioning the Leverhulme team to take soil and environmental samples in the summer of 1990. Likewise, Mike Hodder, then with Sandwell Metropolitan Borough, was one of the first district curators to realise the potential of this research. Early in 1991 he authorised work at Oak House, West Midlands, where soil analysis, and pollen and environmental sampling all made worthwhile contributions to the results (Ponsford 1992, 134).

The National Trust, which had experimented with garden archaeology at Biddulph Grange, Staffordshire, in 1988, was also keen to try the Leverhulme approach. Environmental sampling at Hanbury Hall, Worcestershire, in 1991 produced worthwhile results (Currie 1996a). This was followed by the Hampshire Gardens Trust at Leigh Park, near Portsmouth in 1992 (Currie 1995b). Once again the environmental results helped interpret the garden layout. The Leigh Park site was a particularly notable landmark in garden archaeology in that it showed that successful excavation strategies could be devised for 'informal' garden sites covering hundreds of hectares. Prior to this, many non-archaeologists had voiced the opinion that the discipline could only be expected to work efficiently within formal gardens laid out on geometric principles.

The largest project during the 1990s was at Hampton Court. Here, for the first time, total excavation of a garden was undertaken in order to achieve a single period restoration. This was not without some controversy (Currie 1996b), but the results were visually impressive. They showed, once more, that considerable garden remains can survive more recent changes (Dix and Parry 1995).

As garden archaeology matures, it is learning to take a more considered approach to its sites. Garden restorers appear to be learning to pace their programmes more. Not unexpectedly, it is to the National Trust that many now look to lead the way. Projects like that at Stowe, Buckinghamshire (Marshall 2002), are taking advantage of the new

BISHOP BURTON COLLEGE

Figure 4: Excavation of the excedara *at Painswick, Glos (shown in bottom centre.)*
(Copyright Rob Bell)

emphasis on archaeology to produce projects in which the discipline is being success-fully integrated. Here the emphasis is not so much on single-period restorations, but on an integration of research on the gardens with that of the houses and with the broad landscape settings.

In the meantime archaeology has continued to produce meaningful results on smaller scale projects, such as at Bescot Hall, Staffordshire (Locock 1993a), The Wakes, Selborne, Hampshire (Currie 1995c), and various garden buildings at Painshill, Surrey (Howes 1991). The restoration of specific features has also been important, like the cascade at Gnoll, Neath, Port Talbot (formerly Glamorgan) (Currie *et al* 1994) and the shell house at Newhailes, Edinburgh (see case study in Chapter 15).

More recently the use of garden archaeology has begun to filter down into developer led projects. Since the implementation of PPG16 (DoE 1991), the onus has been to require developers to pay for archaeological recording on sites to be disturbed by development. This has led to a significant increase in the number of garden sites that have been explored by excavation. It is rare that these projects reach publication, but a significant archive of unpublished reports can be found at the National Monuments Record Centre at Swindon. One notable exception to this rule has been at Upper Lodge, in Bushy Park, Greater London, where a long-term development has enabled a comprehensive study of the former water gardens to be undertaken and bought to publication (Currie *et al* 2003).

More recently, British archaeologists, such as Dr Dan Hicks of Bristol University, have exported the techniques developed in the UK to explore the designed landscapes created on plantation estates in the West Indies from the 17th century (Hicks 2002; Hicks 2005 forthcoming). Dr Hicks worked as a student at the Leverhulme research

6

project site of Castle Bromwich Hall, where many of the techniques used in modern garden archaeology were tested and developed.

Finally it should be noted that since the 1980s a number of county-wide and regional studies of historic gardens have been made (see p 167–8), revealing important regional variations in garden design, dictated mainly by local topography and soil conditions. There are clear differences in gardens situated in upland regions of the British Isles from those found in lowland counties. Also the distance from the centre of fashion in London and the Home Counties often dictated the popularity of certain types of garden. It is notable how formal elements tend to survive longer into the 18th century in places like Devon, Wales and Scotland than they do in the counties around London. As Waterhouse (2003) has recently shown in his study of South Devon, terraced gardens seem to have survived here in relatively large numbers throughout the period in the later 18th century when such features were considered unfashionable in the Home Counties.

Three of the earliest studies of gardens of a particular county were undertaken in Northamptonshire (Steane 1977), Oxfordshire (Woodward 1982) and Hampshire (Bilikowski 1983). The latter was partly instrumental in the setting up of England's first county gardens trust, the Hampshire Gardens Trust, which has since done exemplary further work recording gardens in the county. This example has been followed up countrywide and there is now an Association of Gardens Trusts to oversee and coordinate the work of the various individual trusts. Many county and regional surveys not cited in the Section notes below are listed under Further Reading for guidance in this area.

(See end of Section for notes)

7

Chapter 2: Garden design: a historical perspective

It is not the purpose of this chapter to give a detailed analysis of the development of garden design over the ages. It is only intended here to give a broad summary of the development of gardens within the Western European cultural orbit. Such gardens have clearly been influenced by developments outside of Europe, but, in general, they follow a pattern that conforms to the social and political evolution of Western European society. This development has also transferred itself to the former colonies of the major European powers, and gardens in North American, the Caribbean and elsewhere largely follow trends that reflect Western European cultural values. Further information on a number of the gardening terms used here can be found in Symes (1993).

The earliest gardens developed in the Middle East and around the Mediterranean Sea. The famous hanging gardens of Babylon suggest that gardens built to reflect the power and status of the owner extend well back into the centuries before Christ. Little is known about the detailed nature of this legendary Mesopotamian garden, but its very name suggests that it was designed around a series of terraces or different levels, a feature that repeats itself time and time again in the history of garden design. Another clear trait of this garden and its contemporaries must have been water. To introduce it into the garden was essential to grow the plants that made up the design (Dalley 1993, 5). In a land surrounded by desert, the manipulation of water was a clear statement of man's power over nature. This is another characteristic that returns frequently throughout the ages in garden design. There are few notable historic gardens that do not have water features as important elements within them. Thus fountains and ornamental pools appear in the earliest gardens. In the earliest civilisations, centred on the Middle East, there could be no clearer expression of wealth and status than to use the region's most precious commodity, water, in wasteful and ostentatious display. Peoples surrounded by desert could not fail to be impressed by gardens that incorporated watery elements.

Later Classical civilisations were much influenced by Middle Eastern precedents, and many of their features were borrowed and developed to suit more fertile countries. The Romans seem to have inherited the earlier reverence for water, and water features were very much a part of Roman gardens. The terrain of Italy also suited the laying out of terraced gardens on different levels. Thus were these features passed into the Western European cultural databank. A number of Roman writers talk of the way the contemporary aristocracy incorporated ponds and water features into their gardens. Thus it is that fishponds are found in Roman garden designs fulfilling a largely ornamental role, with the fish within them being kept as high status food or pets, rather than for profit. The Roman writer, Marcus Terentius Varro (116–27 BC), bemoans the ostentations of the Republican Roman aristocracy. He says that once fishponds were made by the '… common folk, and [were] not unprofitable' but in more recent times they have come to '… appeal to the eye rather than the purse, and exhaust the pouch of the owner rather than fill it' (Hooper 1934, 522–3). Cicero (106–43 BC) sneered at those that followed the fashion of making such ponds on their estates, and 'who think they can touch the sky with their finger, if they have barbed mullets in their ponds which are tame enough to come when called' (ibid, 525n).

The archaeological remains of some of these ponds in Italy are discussed by Higginbotham (1997), whereas Zeepvat (1988) summarises their discovery in Britain. The terrace and the water feature were therefore two of the earliest elements of garden design that would continue to influence the development of designed landscape in the subsequent two thousand years of Western civilisation.

Cunliffe's (1971) excavation of the Roman palace at Fishbourne has shown how the Roman garden had come to incorporate formal elements in their design by the time they had conquered Britain. Whatever the exact date of the courtyard garden he found there, it is reasonable to assume that its design was influenced by that prevailing in Italy from at least the early 1st century AD. Formal arrangements of box hedging, set within a square or rectangular area, has become a feature of many gardens right up to the present day. Smaller villas in England, such as Frocester, Gloucestershire and Bancroft, Buckinghamshire, have also produced archaeological evidence for gardens (Zeepvat 1991). At Gorhambury, Hertfordshire and Rivenhall, Essex, villas have been found to lie within deliberately-designed landscapes incorporating vistas, landmarks, and avenues of trees (Neal *et al* 1990; Rodwell & Rodwell 1986). The remains of garden plants found during excavations at Silchester and Caerwent are suggestive that gardens were present in urban contexts (Dickson 1994, 49–50). Although work on the form of Roman gardens is in its infancy in Britain more research has been done in the European context (MacDougall & Jashemski 1981; Farrar 1998).

What happened to garden design during the Dark Ages in Europe is uncertain, but there is good reason to suppose that many of the elements of Roman gardens continued to be used and adapted. In England, where there was a clear break in many Classical traditions, little is known about Saxon gardens. When the Normans conquered the country in 1066, they were quick to reintroduce elements of Classical culture that had been lost. Thus fishponds were reintroduced after a lapse of many centuries. However, one should not be misled by antiquarian ideas of producing food for Lent in this reintroduction. The fishpond in medieval times came to be seen as an expression of status, and the fish within them were reserved strictly for special occasions (Currie 1989). The fishpond in medieval England was more than a simple receptacle for high status food items, it was often the central pivot of medieval designed landscape.

It is only in relatively recent times that we have come to appreciate fully the complexity and symbolism in medieval garden and landscape design (Everson 1991). For many years, scholars followed a purely art historical approach, examining pictures, whose deliberately distorted views were designed to cram more into the picture than true perspective would allow, and concluded that medieval garden design was based on the small enclosed space. Many historical books on the subject inadvertently tend to reinforce these views (eg Harvey 1981). Recent work has rapidly advanced our perceptions of medieval gardens. Just as the post-medieval design incorporated some small enclosures as part of often vast panoramas of variously designed elements, so enclosures were only a part of the overall medieval design. These designs incorporated enclosures of various sizes around the aristocratic residence, before breaking out into the surrounding countryside with a series of moats and ponds, spreading further still to the park pale of extensive deer parks. Thus when 'Capability' Brown introduced the 'revolutionary' concept of the landscaped park to the English countryside in the later 18th century, all the elements he used could have been found in the designed landscapes of medieval England. A central element was often water, both for Brown and the medieval aristocrat.

The complexity of medieval landscaping involving water can be seen at a number of sites. Two of the best known to be published are Bodiam Castle, Sussex (Taylor *et al* 1990) and Kenilworth Castle, Warwickshire (Everson 1991, 9; Johnson 2002, 136–42) (see Plate 1), but there are many other cases unpublished. Fieldwork in the last twenty years has shown that these complex designs can be found throughout the English landscape (Everson 1991, 9–12). Designs without water features are rarer, but not entirely unknown, such as the landscape centred on Ludgershall Castle, Wiltshire – apparently designed to enhance views into the surrounding park (Everson 2003, 29–31). Launceston Castle, Cornwall, has recently been interpreted as another landscape designed to create views from castle to park and vice-versa (Herring 2003, 47–48). The example of Middleham Castle in Yorkshire shows how elements of the building design were linked to the views of its landscaped garden, park, and lakes (Taylor 2000).

The medieval design, in broad terms, seems to move from a loose collection of geometric enclosures nearest the residence with increasing variety as the design moves outwards. The inner areas were often enclosed within a moat, which, although having defensive elements, often enclosed areas and features with no defensive purpose. Beyond the moat there are often a series of water features, usually based on contour ponds, and tending to form naturalistic shapes. These ponds are often huge, covering many hectares. Their sheer size prevents them from forming easily managed fish producing units. The shape and form of the ponds are often highly contrived. At Bodiam they led the visitor on a path to show the castle off to its best effect (Taylor *et al* 1990; Johnson 2002).

This is also the case at the bishop of Winchester's palace at Bishop's Waltham. Here the designer did not choose to place the dam between the two large fishponds, covering ten hectares between them, in the most utilitarian place, as he could so easily have done. Instead the dam was built opposite the SW corner of the moated palace. Any travellers coming to the town of Bishop's Waltham from the west were forced to divert all around the upper pond to cross at the dam. They were then obliged to follow the road along a causeway between the pond and the moat. In so doing they passed the full length of the best range of the palace, passing first the bishop's three-storey apartments, then the prodigious great hall, and finally the massive kitchen that the bishop required to cater for his important guests and their retinues.[2]

Such a layout cannot be coincidental. The scene proclaims the power and wealth of the bishop to all who pass, both in the sumptuousness of his buildings, and in his ability to flood good land just to create this effect. The bishops of Winchester had 700 acres of ponds on their various estates. They were rarely utilised to their full extent as fishponds. In 1393 all of these ponds appear to have been fished just once, and that was to provide high status freshwater fish for the visit of Richard II to Winchester (Currie 1988a). These ponds were created to make statements about the bishop's status, and although many of them make little aesthetic or utilitarian sense to garden designers today, they were designed largely for effect. As Cicero's Roman aristocracy, the bishops of Winchester built fishponds mainly for the impact they had on the eye of the beholder. By any definition, this is a 'designed landscape', one made to have a desired effect.

Figure 5: Bishop's Waltham Palace, Hants: the remains of the bishop of Winchester's extensive palace were set in an elaborate designed landscape. Here is the view travellers from Winchester would be greeted with as the road from that town swept around the pond to force all comers to pass the full length of the best range and marvel at the wealth and power of these prince-bishops.

Another medieval garden at nearby St Cross Hospital, Winchester, demonstrates the extensive nature of gardens that were not linked to extensive ponds. Even so, a crucial element of the gardens of this institution was a water channel that the master of the hospital paid the bishop three shillings per annum to divert through the garden. This channel formed earthworks that have a moated form, enclosing a space of about 1.5 hectares. It is uncertain if all four sides of the 'moat' were in existence at the same time, but nevertheless they form the most obvious survival of the earthworks today. A survey of 1401 lists the gardens associated with the hospital. A considerable portion of these were orchards, such as the 'north garden' (Currie 1998a). However, these should not be seen simply as orchards, as the latter were clearly a composite part of the medieval concept of a garden, and often incorporated other elements beneath the trees as is described in Piero de Crescenzi's contemporary treatise on the subject. Crescenzi clearly shows that people of high status were expected to have many hectares of ground laid out as gardens (Calkins 1986), further showing that the antiquarian/art historical idea of medieval gardens being small enclosed spaces is only a partial view.

The medieval deer park was very much part of contemporary designed landscape. Although it had utilitarian purposes, such as the supply of venison and timber, it was traditionally considered that they were 'beautiful landscapes' designed for pleasure. Like fishponds, they performed the function of announcing the owner's high status, and in their heyday, around 1300, it has been estimated that there were around 3,200 parks in England alone (Rackham 1986).

Although some medieval deer parks were disparked in the post-medieval period, many merely changed their form and function to accommodate a wider range of land uses. Many post-medieval parks combined timber production alongside deer keeping, and even arable cultivation could be found in some. This is well demonstrated in a map of 1586 depicting the Tudor park at Hursley, Hampshire. This was one of the medieval bishops of Winchester's deer parks, but by the late 16th century it had been divided into a number of compartments containing different land uses. In the centre of the park a Tudor mansion called the 'Great Lodge' had been erected. This park continued in its compartmented form into the 20th century with the mansion being rebuilt in the 1720s following its acquisition by the Heathcote family (Ponsford forthcoming).

A significant number of new parks were also created during the Tudor period, particularly following the Dissolution of the Monasteries, when a vigorous land market was created by the confiscation of monastic estates. Perhaps the best known Tudor creations are the parks associated with Hampton Court, Greater London. As well as the Home Park, Henry VIII (1509–47) took over some former land of the Knights Hospitallers to the north and created Bushy Park. Both Home and Bushy Park evolved to include ornamental features (canals, avenues etc) that were part of the greater designed landscape of both the royal palace and the two lodges in Bushy Park (Currie *et al* 2003). Other new parks created around this time include Holdenby (Northants), Dyrham (Glos), Compton Wynyates and Charlecote (both Warks).

Garden historians once believed that Tudor and early Stuart gardens were also based on the same sort of small enclosure that was erroneously thought to dominate medieval design. Thus Tudor garden design for much of the 20th century has been seen as represented by the knot garden. These were often small rectangular areas infilled with formal designs of plants and coloured earths. How such gardens were perceived can be seen in the reconstructed knot garden at the Tudor House in Southampton, Hampshire (Anthony 1991, 78). There is little wrong with this design in its context of a small urban garden, but such forms should not be seen to represent the only, or even the dominant form of 16th-century garden design. Like medieval gardens, recent fieldwork has come to show that Tudor gardens could also be vast designed areas, incorporating extensive enclosures and intricate water features alongside the smaller 'knotted' areas.

Many of the more startling of these designs are relatively late in the Tudor period, or are of early Stuart date, such as Lyveden New Bield, Northamptonshire (Brown & Taylor 1973) or Tackley in Oxfordshire (Whittle & Taylor 1994). It is unlikely that these were a late development in the 16th century, with smaller knots dominating the early period. Both Lyveden and Tackley incorporate substantial watery elements in their design, and it is unlikely that the type of garden popular throughout the medieval period was suddenly swept away, only to be followed by similar types of design in the late 16th century. Recent fieldwork is beginning to establish that late Tudor and Stuart gardens evolved from the medieval design. The broader palette provided by the medieval deer park began to show increasing changes in the Tudor period, but the extensive areas taken up by water features and enclosures of various sizes were often still there, only now being developed into more geometric shapes, and moving away from the more naturalistic shapes of the medieval water features (Everson 1991, 12–16).

This is shown relatively early in the expansive earthworks surrounding Raglan Castle, Monmouthshire, described as 'Renaissance' by Whittle (1989) but combining

Figure 6: Drottningholm Palace, Stockholm, Sweden. At the far north of formal gardens but unmistakably in the French style by Andre le Notre. (Copyright Iain Soden)

medieval elements such as the naturalistic lake, with an increasing formality in an early water *parterre* and terraces. By the early 17th century the medieval informality of water features had been largely supplanted by formality, particularly on new sites, although older sites, like Raglan, were often obliged by convenience to incorporate informal lakes and ponds. A good example of this stricter formality can be seen in the early Stuart garden earthworks at Chipping Campden, Gloucestershire, where terraces, canals and a water *parterre* have many similarities to Raglan, but have managed to formalise the large water features as canals. According to Everson (1989, 118) Chipping Campden was mostly the work of one man, Sir Baptist Hicks, and had been largely completed by 1629. The site is of particular interest as it had been abandoned following the destruction of the house in the English Civil War, and was not rebuilt. Thus earthwork forms that might have been considered of later 17th-century date not many years ago could be shown to be somewhat earlier. Further early sites of this nature have since been discovered (Everson 1991) to reinforce the idea that high quality Renaissance style gardens have survived more widely than had been previously thought from documentary and art-historical sources only (Strong 1979).

Cunliffe (1971) has shown how geometric design was part of Roman design, but we do not know if these gardens were merely the inner portions, as they were in medieval designs. It is possible that there was always a formal element in historic gardens, but from the Tudor period, this began to spread out from the inner core. In the first decade of the 18th century, the inner enclosures often grew larger, becoming increasingly formal. Small knots gave way to more extensive geometric designs called *parterres*.

13

Figure 7: Shaw House, Newbury, Berkshire: An earthwork viewing terrace survives around two sides of the earlier formal gardens to allow the geometric designs to be best appreciated. Possibly 17th- or early 18th-century in date.

Terraces began to spread outwards into the middle landscape. Walled enclosures became larger, often incorporating the *parterres* and terraces entirely, as at the late formal garden at Castle Bromwich, West Midlands (Currie & Locock 1993a). Parkland began to become popular once more, but unlike the informal medieval park, with its naturalistic appearance of randomly distributed grassland, trees and woods, the parkland that accompanied later 17th and early 18th century landscapes was divided up by extensive straight avenues of trees and formal vistas cut through the countryside to afford highly contrived views.

Contemporaries came to associate such rigid formality with the absolutist power of the French kings. The most admired of these formal landscapes ornamented the French king's palace at Versailles, just outside Paris. Initially courtiers of Stuart kings like Charles II (reigned 1660–85), and James II (reigned 1685–88), admired and copied this style. After the deposition of James and the accession of William and Mary in 1689, attitudes slowly began to change in England. Formality in landscaping was increasingly seen as a 'French' style (Fig 6), and a movement grew that tried to develop a purely English style, particularly as England set on a path that led to almost one hundred and thirty years of intermittent war with France.

Amongst the early opponents of formality in gardening were the essayist, Joseph Addison (1672–1719), and the poet, Alexander Pope (1688–1744). They grew to despise formality as unnatural, and urged garden designs to seek out the 'genius of the place', making gardens appear more natural. Initially this was largely superficial, and many of the earliest gardens that sought to move away from strict formality were

14

Figure 8: The Vyne, Basingstoke (Hants): a summer house dating from the early 17th century, the sole survivor of the earlier formal gardens

largely formal themselves. However, the change was gradual, and over the first 50 years of the 18th century, garden design slowly dispensed with elements of the more rigid formality that prevailed in the opening years of that century. It is not possible to identify the exact moment of change, and many of the earliest designs in the new fashion still look largely formal to modern eyes, even though the basis for change can be detected by careful scrutiny. It has been considered that 'the first movement away from an entirely regular conception of garden design' occurred in The Grove at Melborne Hall, Derbyshire. Here, irregularly aligned alleys with circular spaces at their intersections containing formal fountain pools were new in England when it was laid out in 1705. Yet, even this 'innovation' was initially borrowed from France, seen as the home of the formal garden to many British eyes. Both Le Notre and Mansard had developed this technique, particularly at Marly, from 1696 (Hussey 1967, 61).

Designers such as Charles Bridgeman (?–1725) and then William Kent (1685–1748) are thought to be the pioneers of the purely 'English' movement away from formality. Many garden historians consider the most important element in this change was the 'invention' of the ha-ha, a form of sunken fence, which allowed the countryside beyond the garden to be drawn into the landscape. These appear from *c* 1700, but were popularised by Bridgeman. The deconstruction of formal landscapes was continued by Kent, but even so, many of his early works still displayed elements of formality.

Places like Claremont, Surrey (Fig 10), show how landscape design moved from formal to informal by gradual degrees. Both Bridgeman and Kent worked on this garden (Fig 9). Bridgeman's changes still incorporated many formal elements that were only slowly, but never entirely, removed by Kent. Thus the plan of the garden by Colin Campbell in *Vitruvius Britannicus* (1725) can be compared with the gradual

Figure 9: Bridgeman's reconstructed amphitheatre at Claremont, Surrey, seen across the later lake

Figure 10: Claremont, Surrey: one of the few examples of a landscape designed by Capability Brown where he had a hand in the design of the new house as well, using his brother-in-law as the architect. Note how the house is typically set on rising ground to get the best views with uninterrupted grass rolling right up to the house.

softening of the harsher lines of the straight vistas and avenues on successive plans by John Rocque, dated 1738, 1750 and c 1770.

Perhaps the finest surviving example of Kent's work is at Rousham in Oxfordshire, but even here he revamped an earlier design by Bridgeman. By the end of Kent's life in 1748, the new style that he had helped to create came to be seen as the 'English' landscape, a name which is universally used to describe informal park-like landscapes today. Nearly everything that is recognised as a feature of this design, shelter belts, clumps of trees and serpentine water features, had been used by Kent, but it was only in the hands of Lancelot 'Capability' Brown (1715–83) that the style became largely standardised.

Nevertheless, even in 1748 there were probably still many more formal gardens in Britain than there were designs in the new style. For example, Sir John Bridgeman was still working on his extended walled formal garden at Castle Bromwich in the period 1730–47 (Currie & Locock 1993, 118). Thus, while an influential minority were creating fashionable designs before 1750, there were still people creating new formal gardens and extending existing ones in the old manner. It seems that these late designs were becoming increasingly spartan in their use of plants, with designs picked out in coloured earths and ornamented with architectural features such as statues and elaborate urns at the expense of the plant content as indicated by archaeology at Castle Bromwich and Tredegar House (Currie & Locock 1997).

Tom Williamson has been prominent amongst historians in noting what archae- ology was beginning to show about later formal gardens. He argues that prior to his collaboration with Anthea Taigel (1993) and the publication of his own work on 18th-century designed landscape (Williamson 1995), garden historians had been prone to write an over-simplified version of garden history during this period that concentrated on major designers and certain famous 'key sites' like Stowe, Rousham and Stourhead that 'repeatedly appear in books on garden history like so many rabbits out of a hat' (*ibid*, 4–5). Yet he considers that if 'we broaden our view... a different picture emerges' whereby the gardens of the early and middle decades of the 18th century are not dominated by the new fashion for informal landscapes, but continue to be dominated by formal (or, as he calls them, 'geometric') gardens (Taigel & Williamson 1993, 48).

These two important publications identify some important characteristics of late formal gardens. In the 1720s and 1730s these often contain wildernesses or groves adjoining the principle vista to the house. Parks were becoming increasingly part of the landscape once more, with vistas radiating through them from the *parterres* and terraces closer to the house (*ibid*, 50–56). This practice, contrary to the writings of earlier garden historians, predominated in the British countryside well into the 1760s, and it was only after this decade that the tide of fashion really turned towards the overwhelming adoption of the informal landscape that has come to be associated with 'Capability' Brown.

At the same time that formal gardens were coming under attack by the new wave of garden aficionados another movement was running parallel with these developments. This was the style that has become known as Rococo. It is not easy to define a Rococo garden as the style was not necessarily applied to the entire garden, but is often restricted to individual buildings or features. Symes (1993, 100) defines it as 'A style characterised in the visual arts by playfulness, elegance, asymmetry and sometimes wilfulness. In English gardens the term may be applied to some smaller gardens of the

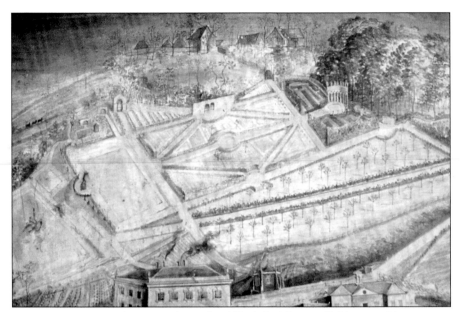

Figure 11: Painting of Painswick garden (Glos), by Thomas Robins c 1750.
(Copyright Rob Bell)

mid-eighteenth century, together with some individual buildings or other features in a larger garden, to demonstrate a light-hearted and fanciful approach which may take advantage of a number of different architectural styles – Gothic, Chinese, rustic.' The name seems to come from the French *rocaille* which means rockwork and *coquille* meaning shell. Thus the principal characteristic of most Rococo gardens and features involves rockwork of some sort or buildings decorated with shellwork or tufa (see Chapter 15).

One of the best known Rococo gardens is the restored design at Painswick, Gloucestershire, created during the 1740s by Benjamin Hyett, a successful burgess of Gloucester, as a country retreat. This garden is characterised by its whimsical garden buildings and irregular path layout. It includes asymmetrical features to be found in later English Landscape gardens but still tends to keep its overall lines straight, rather like many of Bridgeman's designs, such as Claremont. The quirkiness of the design is exemplified in a contemporary painting by Thomas Robins, a topographical artist (Bell 1993).

A number of gardens contain what have been considered Rococo work. Some, such as Bowood (Wilts) and Highclere (Hants), were later worked on by 'Capability' Brown, who left some of these earlier features in place, such as the 'Rococo valley' at Bowood with its rockwork features, grotto tunnels and cascade, or the 'Jackdaw's Castle', now an isolated folly at Highclere. Timothy Mowl (1995) has shown how the present Half Mile Pond at Longleat (Wilts) originated as a Rococo lake, characterised by its double serpentine curve. This was created by Thomas Thynne, the 2nd Viscount Weymouth, between 1733 and 1736 whilst he was under the influence of his wife, Louisa. She was the daughter of Lord Carteret, a supporter of Frederick, Prince of Wales, the latter being an admirer of the Rococo style (*ibid*, 58–9). The sinuosity of the pond was changed by Humphry Repton early in the 19th century, who believed its regular shape exhibited the earlier 'bigotry for serpentine lines' (*op cit*, 64).

Even as Rococo reached its zenith in the 1740s and 1750s, so Lancelot 'Capability' Brown (1716–83) was beginning his work that would transform many of England's best known country estates. A Brownian park, and its many imitators, is instantly recognised. The house is situated on higher ground to afford the best views. Earlier houses were often low-lying so that they could be moated or utilise local water supplies. Houses in Brownian parks were set in rolling grassland, with no walled enclosures or *parterres* around them. Where a kitchen garden was required to supply produce, it was hidden away behind trees in the park, some distance from the house. Within the parkland surrounding the house were strategically placed clumps of trees, seemingly natural, but often placed to frame a view. In the middle distance was the serpentine lake, built so that one end could not be seen from the other, giving the illusion that it was a far bigger piece of water. In the distance was a shelter belt of trees, placed to hide the boundary of the park, so that the visitor was further deluded into thinking the park was bigger than in reality. Paths and carriage roads, where they were required, wound their way through the landscape, so that few straight lines could be found. Garden design had gone from one extreme of rigid formality to another of strict informality. Whereas the formality of the garden at the beginning of the 18th century had taken 2000 years to evolve gradually, so the informal reaction was accomplished in less than seventy.[3] The 'English Landscape' did not confine itself to the British Isles, before the 18th century was over, it had spread across Europe, and could be found as far afield as Sweden (Phibbs 1993) and Russia (Cross 1991).

There are many useful biographies of the leading designers of the 18th century, including Dorothy Stroud's works on Brown (Stroud 1975) and Humphry Repton (Stroud 1962). Willis' study (1978) of the enigmatic Charles Bridgeman, a man who we do not even have a birth date for, is of particular interest. For one of the less well-known designers Colwell (1986) has published a preliminary account of the work of Richard Woods (?1716–93).

Despite the dominance Brown had in the period 1750–83 in landscape design, there were still gentleman amateurs who preferred to create their own designs. Amongst the most influential of these were by William Shenstone at the Leasowes, West Midlands (created between 1743 and 1763), Charles Hamilton at Painshill in Surrey (1738–73), and Henry Hoare II at Stourhead, Wiltshire (1744–70). All began their work before Brown came to prominence, and showed greater individuality than the majority of Brown's designs, which tended to be carried out to a formula. It might be noted that all three of these 'amateur' designs relied heavily on water features. Both Painshill (Howes 1991) and Stourhead (Woodbridge 1982) were laid out around a lake, whereas the Leasowes was based on two converging stream valleys, with a succession of ponds, rills, and cascades set along them (Gallagher 1996). Brown also had rivals in the professional field, and, although these were nowhere near as popular, there are landscapes of note that can be attributed to them. Richard Woods and William Emes (1730–1803) were among his more successful rivals.

Brown's work was continued by Humphry Repton (1752–1818), his best known successor. Repton's work tended to be less manicured than Brown's, often introducing 'wilder' elements into his designs in keeping with contemporary notions of 'picturesque' scenery. Towards the end of his career he began reintroducing some formal

Figure 12: Fitzwarren Park, Surrey: the remains of an abandoned and previously unknown Pulhamite 'rock' garden in the grounds of this 19th-century 'Gothick' mansion.

elements around the house, such as flower gardens and planted balustrades, the latter being little more than small terraces. He even reintroduced the *parterre*, considered by early protagonists of the naturalist landscaping as anathema.

Once Repton had reintroduced the *parterre*, the flood gates opened for the reintroduction of diversity to garden design. The rest of the 19th and 20th century saw garden design becoming less rigid in the fashion that it was acceptable to follow, and it became increasingly acceptable to mix styles. The early 19th century was dominated by the writings of John Claudius Loudon (1783–1843), whose gardening encyclopaedias formed the text books followed by the increasing number of amateur designers. Although Loudon was initially a follower of the informal 'Picturesque' school of landscape design, he slowly modified his views to recognise the validity of formal designs in appropriate circumstances. Loudon also popularised the 'gardenesque', a term he coined in 1832, for gardens where the plants themselves became the focus, as opposed to being forced into an artificial design (Symes 1993, 54). A good study of Loudon's contribution to landscape design can be found in Simo (1988).

One of Loudon's major contributions was the introduction of the popular gardening magazine. He edited the *Gardener's Magazine* from 1826 to 1843, the first periodical of its kind, and this allowed him and the editors of successor magazines in the 19th century to promote their views on garden design. It was during this period that formal revivalist gardens in the Italian style began to gain popularity. The architect Charles Barry (1795–1860) was a major exponent of the style, producing memorable designs comprising architectural terracing with elaborate balustrades, staircases, urns and fountains at places such as Trentham Park (Staffs) and Cliveden (Bucks). Another well-known exponent of formal revivalism was Barry's contemporary, William Nesfield (1793–1881). He is best known for utilising designs that he found in 16th and 17th-century garden books to imitate *parterres* of the period. His work can be seen at Holkham and Bickling Hall in Norfolk and at Kew Gardens, Surrey. The horticultural journalist, Henry Noel Humphrey (1807–79), wrote approvingly of Barry's style in Loudon's periodical (Leathlean 1995, 178), and thus helped to promote its popularity. Later in the 19th century, he was to write for William Robinson (1838–1936) whilst the latter was editor of *Garden*. By this time Humphrey's views had moved with the times, and he was able to support Robinson's enthusiasm for 'wild gardens', where garden design, once more, tried to look as natural as possible by incorporating mixtures of wild and cultivated plants, not in formal beds, but scattered around 'naturally' amongst a backdrop of grass, similarly to that found in a wild flower meadow today.

The popularity of formal revivalism was much helped by the massive building programme in the 19th century of suburban middle-class villas. These homes of the minor gentry and professional classes could not afford the expansive landscaping undertaken by Brown and Repton, and were obliged to tailor their gardens to their more restricted grounds. These ranged from a hectare or less to fifteen hectares, and usually had formal elements around the house, with informal shrubberies expanding outwards to the boundary. These gardens were particularly suited to 'gardenesque' ideas whereby individual trees were planted in the outer grounds for their horticultural and arboricultural interest. Such ideas were particularly encouraged by the large number of exotic specimens that were being introduced to the UK and Europe at this

Figure 13: The War Memorial Park, Basingstoke: a fine example of a late 19th-century bandstand (not in situ) in a public park that developed from an earlier designed landscape belonging to a minor country house on the outskirts of the town. Subsequent suburban spread has put the park in the town centre.

time as a result of colonial ventures that encouraged plant collectors to visit distant lands and bring new specimens back with them. The survival of exotic specimens can be extremely useful in providing a *terminus post quem* on many otherwise poorly documented sites of this period.

The mixture of styles continued throughout the 19th century.[4] Theme gardens also flourished at this time. One of the earliest of these was the work of the much travelled Sir George Staunton (1781–1859). Between 1820 and 1850 he created a designed landscape covering about 400 hectares that included an American garden, a Dutch garden and a Chinese (water) garden, as well as Turkish, Gothic and Regency Model Farm elements at Leigh Park, near Havant, Hampshire (Gladwyn 1992). Japanese gardens were created at Newark Abbey, Nottinghamshire, and Tatton Park, Cheshire, both set as distinct areas within a larger design.

During the 19th century the public park began to become popular. Such parks were symbols of municipal pride, and most large towns had them by 1900. Many saw these as an instrument of social reform whereby the working classes could have access to pleasure grounds similar to the private parks of the upper classes. These first appeared in areas of the greatest concentrations of working class populations such as Derby, Liverpool and Manchester, which had public parks laid out from the 1840s (Taylor 1995). Running parallel with this was the idea of the cemetery garden, one of the many ideas promoted by Loudon. Examples can be found at Woking, Surrey and Abney Park, London.

The later 19th and early 20th century saw the rise in popularity of the rock garden (Fig 12). These were made fashionable on a large-scale by the Pulham family from the 1840s. They created large-scale rockwork using a clever mix of cement to imitate stone. Many of their designs were so well-executed they were known to fool experienced geologists. The Pulhams created rock gardens throughout the country well into the 1920s, and still have their imitators today. Both Sandringham and Buckingham Palace have Pulhamite rock gardens in their grounds (Festing 1984). An elaborate Pulhamite-style rock garden has recently been restored at Warsash, Hampshire, by the local authority. This covers a sizable area and incorporates a series of rocky rills, ponds and a cave.

Archaeology has now been used in most of the garden types described above. It has been used not only to investigate earlier garden designs of royalty and the aristocracy at places like Hampton Court and Castle Bromwich Hall, but also to inform management decisions in public parks and in 20th-century gardens. At Bantock Park, West Midlands, the design of this Edwardian villa has been recovered to enable the public park there, now managed by Wolverhampton Borough Council, to be restored. The author has published the results of an archaeological assessment of the War Memorial Park in Basingstoke, Hampshire (Fig 13) as part of a municipal Lottery Fund project, showing how it was converted from a modest suburban private estate initiated in the early 19th century into a public park in the early 20th century (Currie 2001). At Dartington Hall, archaeological techniques have contributed towards decision making in this evolving garden. Although Dartington contains many medieval and later elements, much of the present garden was redesigned in the 20th century by the Elmhirst family using modern designers such as H Avery Tipping and Percy Cane (Currie 2003).

In a review of Brown's *Garden Archaeology* (1991), Turner (1992) called for a look at the archaeology of the more humble garden to redress the balance of interest in the country house garden. There has been some progress on this front, such as the archaeological work on the gardens that were worked by paupers at the Southwell Workhouse in Nottinghamshire, and the garden designed by the poor country curate, Gilbert White (1720–93), who became posthumously famous for his pioneering naturalists' book, *The Natural History of Selborne* (Currie 1995c). The work at these sites has demonstrated how the less wealthy managed their gardens in the second half of the 18th century (see case studies).

SECTION NOTES

1   This chapter has extended on an earlier essay by the author and Martin Locock (Currie & Locock 1995).
2   This is the author's interpretation of this site. It has not been previously published.
3   Moggridge's (1987, 108–11) work at Blenheim, Oxon, has shown that Brown's design here was based on complex geometry with clumps of trees and other features being sited to afford intersecting views from a number of points along a carriage drive through the park.
4   For a detailed overview of Victorian gardening see Brent Elliott (1986), *Victorian gardens* London: Batsford.

SECTION 2: METHODS

Chapter 3: undertaking documentary research

The interpretation of historic gardens has sometimes resulted in differences between art historians, garden historians and archaeologists. If a feature is documented but cannot be found by archaeology, then it is tempting for non-archaeologists to consider that there is an inherent fault in the discipline itself or in the particular excavator. Likewise, if the archaeologists find features that are not documented, then getting these features taken into the chronology of the garden can often be problematic. Truly multidisciplinary approaches try to overcome the inherent difficulties of specific methodologies, as can a willingness on all sides to confront the unexpected.

A regular problem with the documentation of historic gardens is that features that appear to be documented, particularly in plans and illustrations, were not necessarily the features that were actually built. Pictures of gardens were often idealised to please the owner. Plans were sometimes proposals that were either not carried out at all or else were modified to greater or lesser extent once work commenced.

Even when plans can be shown to have been carried out, for the most part healthy scepticism will seldom go amiss over the detail. Thus at Hanbury Hall, Worcestershire, an early 18th -century formal garden was seemingly well documented by a

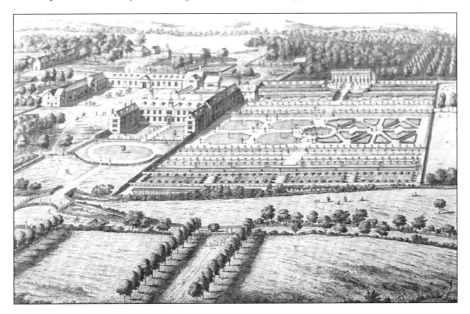

Figure 14: Southwick Park, Hampshire: a formal terraced garden from an early 18th-century Kip print. This is a good example of how misleading such illustrations can be. The paddock behind the house with the dovecote-like building in the far corner was the site of monastic fishponds that had a continuous life through to the present. At the time the print was made there was an elaborate water garden here, the earthworks of which still survive, but this is not shown.

27

contemporary plan and a detailed print (Fig 15) showing a perspective view by the normally reliable Dougharty brothers of Worcester. Careful examination of these documents showed a discrepancy in the positioning of two small pavilions to the north of the main *parterre* (Currie 1996a, fig 3 & 4). The print showed the pavilions parallel to the E–W axis of the *parterre*, the plan showed them set diagonally. Excavation proved the plan to be correct (see Plate 2), but what if only the print had survived? It could have been suggested that the pavilions had been rebuilt, and archaeology had failed to recognise this change. As it was, the print was shown to be in error because both print and plan were drawn at the same time by the same artist to complement each other. This example shows clearly that such mistakes can be made. There are numerous examples of archaeology not being able to match the detail of 18th-century illustrations, but in most cases the corroborating evidence that the print was wrong did not exist. It is necessary to recognise that the failure to match the archaeology to plans and illustrations does not necessarily mean it has failed to find all the details or is wrong.

Another example of documentary and archaeological coordination can be illustrated by the excavation of the grottoes either side of the cascade at Upper Lodge, Bushy Park, Greater London. Here there are a number of illustrations of the grottoes, including two paintings and a drawing. However the archaeology only found a very simple and shallow alcove on the site of one of the grottoes that seemed to contradict the illustrative material, the latter showing the grottoes as elaborate cave-like features. A letter from Samuel Molyneux, written in 1714, clarified the anomaly by explaining that the cave effect was created by paintings placed at the back of a shallow alcove (Currie *et al* 2003, 94–95).[1]

This is a rare documented example of how tricks of perspective were used to create illusions in historic gardens. These examples act as warnings on the dangers of taking documentary sources too literally. It is imperative that the sources are regarded objectively, and that the potential for misinterpretation, such as those outlined above, is recognised.

To undertake proper research on an historic garden one should look at as many original sources as possible. Even where a site is covered by good secondary sources,

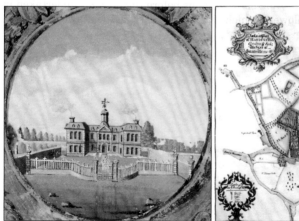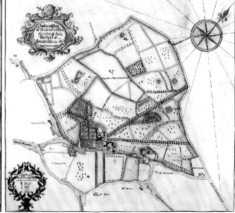

Figure 15: Hanbury Hall print and plan

these need to be checked, as the study of documents is fraught with dangers of misinterpretation. Such errors are often unintentional, particularly where a restoration programme is involved in bringing a garden to a specific date. On such occasions there is a temptation to interpret ambivalent documents in a way that will suit the restoration plan. Researchers should take care to state clearly where there are elements of doubt in interpretation.

The most likely location of historic records on any garden is the local record office. This is usually the county record office, but it can occasionally be a city record office. Such places usually hold detailed catalogues of the documents they hold. Sometimes the records for a garden have been retained in private hands. Some estates, as at Longleat, Wilts, have such detailed records that they employ their own archivist. Access to such documents can often be obtained by appointment, although this may involve a charge. Other private records have no official admission, but a polite letter explaining the purpose of the research can often obtain access. The present author has yet to be refused sight of private documents, but then it is rare that such applications have to be made. The greater proportion of all estate or family papers can be found in local record offices.

In the last few years, a range of Internet resources have been developed that greatly simplify the task of locating relevant archive material. These include the National Register of Archives (UK), the National Archives A2A (England), Archives Network Wales and SCAN (Scotland).[2]

For historic gardens, the most important documents are often maps, and these are usually consulted first. Sometimes a detailed sequence of estate maps survive. For example, an excellent series of maps survive for the royal palace at Hampton Court and its adjoining lodges, the latter having substantial gardens in their own right, as has recently been shown by the work at Upper Lodge (*ibid*). More often one is obliged to seek out more general maps. The earliest of any scale are county maps produced in the 18th and early 19th centuries. County maps before 1750 are rarely of sufficient scale to be useful for gardens, but hereafter more detailed maps can be found. In the counties around London, John Rocque produced a series of maps between about 1740 and 1768 that show excellent detail of historic gardens. Most of these were drawn at a scale of two inches to one mile, and show gardens before the changes undertaken by Capability Brown and his followers, which swept many early gardens away. There are other counties that have maps almost equal to Rocque's masterpieces, such as Yeakel and Gardener's later 18th-century map of the county of Sussex.

Should it be found that the site being researched is poorly served by county or estate maps, the tithe map will usually show it as it was in the 1840s. The majority of English parishes are served by tithe maps, often at scales not equalled until the 1st edition Ordnance Survey 25 inch maps of the 1870s were published. Tithe maps are often highly informative, giving detailed plans of the garden or designed landscape. The only problem with this source is that the date, usually in the early 1840s, is after the Brownian period, and so there is a good chance that fashion has swept away many pre-1750s gardens. Nevertheless there are still clues to be found. Despite the opinion that Brown and his contemporaries destroyed everything wherever they were employed, their alterations to earlier layouts were seldom entire. Compromises were frequently made when dictated by site practicalities. Thus at Blenheim Palace, Oxfordshire, the great lake laid out by Brown utilises the same part of the valley as an earlier canal. Air photographs have shown that part of the outline of that canal can still be seen in the bed of the present lake (Green & Bond 1987, 81–83). Sometimes the tithe map will still contain clues that show where part of an earlier feature has been retained. At North Stoneham, Hampshire, Brown used the line of a medieval deer park pale to site a ha-ha. The entire outline of this earlier park can still be traced on the tithe map, although it needed the aid of fieldwork and earlier written descriptions to confirm this (Currie 1997a).

Large-scale Ordnance Survey maps, at 6 and 25 inches to the mile, appear from the late 1860s, and cover most of the UK. The first four editions of these maps are the most useful for our purposes. These were mostly issued three or four years either side of the following dates, 1870, 1896, 1910 and 1933. They often show a good sequence of change, although in the inter-war years of 1918–39 many country house gardens were neglected, and often had features removed to save on the cost of maintenance. The inter-war years were a period of great hardship to the aristocracy in the UK, and many had to abandon their family homes to save money. The high maintenance costs of extensive gardens were often the first saving to be made, and in these years so many of our great historic gardens were either lost or seriously depleted. The Ordnance Survey series from 1870 into the 1930s often documents this process.

After maps, estate papers are often the most important sources. These can be patchy in what they record. It is very much a matter of survival, and this is often down to pure chance or the particular interest of specific owner. At The Vyne, Hampshire, there are detailed records of the fishing and repairs that the Chute family carried out on the estate ponds in the second half of the 18th century, but after 1800 the subject is seldom mentioned (Currie 1994a). Likewise at Highclere, Hampshire, there are detailed records of the flowerpots purchased in the early 19th century, but little on this subject before or after (Currie 1993, 231–32). Some estate records contain little about garden work, others contain minute details of plantings. It is never possible to prejudge the outcome of any documentary search. Checking on the references given to the numerous single site historical studies given in journals such as *Garden History* can often give the novice researcher an idea of the type of sources such studies use.

Another useful documentary source can be sale particulars. These are rare before the 18th century, but are increasingly common from 1750 onwards. They can give great detail of the estate grounds, and often conceal a map or plan that is not listed in the normal map catalogue at the given record office. Inventories can also be useful sources. Although these are usually made to detail the contents of the house, they sometimes give the contents of greenhouses, and other garden buildings, in some cases being the only record that such buildings existed. Sometimes they list the moveable items in the gardens, such as statuary, urns, and gates. A recent project undertaken by the author and Sybil Wade on the small, country estate of Priestlands, Hants, discovered an inventory that listed the iron fencing within the grounds. This stated clearly how many lengths of fencing were used in each section, where the gates were, and where each length began and ended, thus enabling a detailed reconstruction of the boundaries within the pleasure grounds of this house. It was signed by Frederick Ellis, an incoming tenant in 1867, and was made to record all the moveable items on the estate at the time he took it over (Currie & Wade 2003).

A source that is frequently overlooked in researching a garden site is gardening magazines. These were popularised by J C Loudon from the 1820s. Although many would see them as secondary sources, they often give a picture of a garden at a specific point in time. From an early date it was quite common for the journalist writing these

Figure 16: Dartington Hall, Devon: an early photography from 1868 shows a formal revivalist garden in the valley below the hall.

magazines to target a specific garden in an early sort of 'how-they-do-it' article. Magazines such as the *Gardeners Chronicle* often give descriptions of gardens as they were in the 19th and early 20th century. From the 1860s they are often illustrated by good photographs, which are another good source, wherever they are found, for gardens. From the later 19th century many country houses, even relatively obscure ones, were given a separate article in *Country Life*. One has to beware of any anecdotal 'history' that is given here as the authors of these articles were often susceptible to the wishes of the garden owners, and repeated myths invented by them as irrevocable fact.[3] A complete index of *Country Life* can be found in the National Monuments Record Centre, Swindon, Wilts. This is also a good source for old photographs of historic gardens.

This chapter has dealt largely with post-medieval sources. Earlier documents relating to gardens are rare, but they exist. A particularly useful source is the treatise. Roman literature is full of works on gardens. The Loeb Library series contains many useful texts on Roman gardens, such as Varro's *Res Rustica* (Hooper 1934). Zeepvat (1991, 53) quotes Pliny in his article on the subject, but there are many others too numerous to mention here. Of the medieval texts, the author's favourite is Piero de Crescenzi's treatise (Calkins 1986), as it so clearly demonstrates that medieval aristocratic gardens could be the extensive designs that landscape archaeology is so frequently revealing. Many historians like to quote Harvey's (1981) overview of the subject, but this should be treated with caution nowadays as it was written before many of the more recent discoveries of extensive garden earthworks, and tends to reinforce the impression, perhaps unintentionally, that medieval gardens were small enclosed spaces. Nevertheless, some of Harvey's work on medieval documents relating to gardens, such as those for the infirmary garden at Westminster Abbey (Harvey 1992) and Thomas Fromond's list of herbs 'necessary for a garden' (Harvey 1989) remain essential reading for those working in this sphere.

(See end of Section for notes)

Chapter 4: Aerial photography

Historic gardens have received much attention from the advocates of aerial photography in the recent past. It is possibly fair to state that it was in the realm of air photography that the present archaeological interest in gardens and designed landscapes had much of its origin. It is generally accepted that Christopher Taylor's, *The archaeology of gardens*, was the first serious book on the subject, and of the 27 photographs illustrating this work, 15 are aerial views. This is not unexpected as Taylor was a member of the Royal Commission on the Historical Monuments of England, who for many years curated one of the nation's most important aerial collections (now held in the National Monuments Record Centre at Swindon, Wilts). Taylor has reinforced his reliance on air photographs as a source in a recent book tracing the history of landscape design from the air (Taylor 1998). Another former Royal Commission employee, Paul Everson, is also one of the most published writers on historic gardens. Again his works (*cf* Everson 1991, 2003) rely heavily on air photographs, both as illustrations of his points and as a way to interpret the gardens and the earthworks that they leave.

There is no doubt, therefore, that air photographs have proved an important source of information on historic gardens. A good air photograph can sometimes give almost as much information as a measured survey, particularly if used with a stereoscope, which enables the earthworks to be seen in relief, giving clearer information on height of banks etc. As well as providing the archaeologist with a ready-made 'plan' view of earthworks air photographs are useful for detecting buried features through crop and parch marks. Such clues to what is beneath the ground can often only be fully appreciated from the air.

For those wishing to commission new aerial photographs, some comment should be made on the respective merits of the different types. Colour photographs often show up more detail, and can sometimes distinguish subtle changes in soil or crop colouration better than monochrome prints. Until recently colour photographs were not favoured by curating bodies as they are not particularly archive-friendly, the colours tending to fade over time. This is why the majority of surveys undertaken until recently were carried out in monochrome. This has changed more recently with the advent of digital photography. This enables both colour and monochrome prints to be taken from the same source. It should be noted that the long-term preservation of digital photographs requires active management to update defunct formats. Nevertheless, the ability to produce prints in any format is an advantage worth consideration.

A similar case can be made for the use of colour slides. These can also be used to produce colour and monochrome prints, with the additional advantage in the slide itself being a relatively archive-friendly 'negative'. In the realm of below-ground excavation, colour slide photography has now entirely replaced colour prints (although this has only become standard since the early 1990s), so there is no reason to see why air photography cannot go the same way. If photographs are required for publication, it is worth noting that most publishers still prefer monochrome prints for black and white illustrations rather than those converted from slides or a digital source.

Figure 17: Castle Bromwich Hall, West Midlands: the walled gardens from the air, with the tree avenue on the western vista extending into the parkland beyond, a ruse typical of late formal gardens whereby views out into the surrounding countryside became increasingly important. View with areas of garden over written.

As well as the format of the film used, it is also necessary to consider the type of photograph to be taken. Most collections contain what are called 'oblique' and 'vertical' photographs. The former are taken at an oblique angle to the site (Fig 18), often to try to take advantage of low-light conditions and the effects of shadow, the latter often throwing earthworks into stronger relief than vertical shots. The

Figure 18: St Cross Hospital, Winchester (Hants), the finest medieval almshouse in England with extensive contemporary records of the medieval gardens (Currie 1998a). An oblique aerial view from the church tower across part of the former medieval gardens showing parch marks (foreground) in the grass and the earthworks of a perimeter ditch in the background.

disadvantage of oblique shots is that the scale of the site furthest from the camera is often distorted, making it difficult to determine the size relationships between different features. This can often be rectified by taking vertical photographs from directly above the site. Many professional surveys take verticals at a set distance above the ground so that the resultant photographs can be used to provide scale plans. Vertical air photography is now an important tool in map-making. Many local councils now commission regular aerial surveys of their entire district. These are usually taken every ten years, the resultant photographs being produced at a scale of 1:10,000.

Even so, obliques have decided advantages over verticals when it comes to highlighting the relief of a site, and in many cases where scale is not the most important issue, they can be preferred as an interpretive tool. Verticals, particularly as the majority are taken at heights too great to enable good detail to be seen, tend to make the site look flat and uninspiring, and a stereoscope is often needed to bring out the site's relief. Although the latter is a useful instrument, it requires much practice to perfect its use, and, even then, photographs viewed under stereoscopic viewers have a tendency to highlight false features that result from the natural topography. It takes years of practice to filter these features, a problem that is less prone to occur when using good oblique views taken in good (low-light) conditions.

In recent years some good results have been obtained using infra-red photography (Wilson 2000, 33–34). The author has no personal experience of this method on garden sites, but he has seen it used to good effect on a Roman site, although, like standard photographs, the infra-red photograph is just as capable of throwing up false features along with the genuine. This method is only really applicable for those with experience.

Weather conditions are a prime factor in obtaining good air photographs. Not only do the light conditions themselves help illuminate aspects of a site by throwing relief-enhancing shadows across it, but a long spell of prolonged dry weather can produce excellent crop- and parch-marks. It is not intended to detail why such conditions produce the results they do as this has been covered elsewhere (Wilson 2000, 38–97). Simply put, lack of rain causes certain features to dry out whereas others will retain moisture. Thus where there is a wall, gravel path, or similar feature, buried beneath the surface, the ground will tend to 'parch' forming a strip of drier ground over a ploughed field, or a stunted growth if there is a crop present. In a pasture field such features will often cause the grass above it to turn yellow. Conversely, if there was a ditch or similar water-holding feature present beneath the ground, the ground will tend to retain moisture causing the area to remain green in pasture, when all around is yellow, or to cause an arable crop to be more lush immediately above it. Many sites reveal a combination of different types of features resulting in a palimpsest of marks that will then require interpretation.

Wilson (1991, 20–1) has commented that gardens have presented a 'special case' in the history of air photographic analysis in that, even when the photographs exist, they have failed to be interpreted correctly. Many 'deserted villages' are now being recognised as manorial garden earthworks. In his words 'Custodians of collections of air-photographs now have the task of reviewing their holdings to see how many examples can be rediscovered that have hitherto been overlooked'. He (*ibid*, 34–5) also puts particular emphasis on the difficulty in distinguishing genuine monastic earthworks from post-Dissolution garden features, as many monasteries were supplanted by a country house that reused part of the earlier buildings.

Air photographs can also be particularly useful in identifying former tree planting holes. These were first drawn to the attention of the author in correspondence with Jim Pickering, who had discovered alignments of such features that he suspected might be late prehistoric ritual alignments (pers comm). Since then the author has seen a number of such features on air photographs on garden sites. Examples are given by Wilson (1991, 31–2; 2000, 189–90), who urges care in their interpretation as tree planting pits can frequently be mistaken for prehistoric domestic pits and vice-versa. A frequent clue to the existence of ornamental planting pits is the regularity of the pattern that they often form, whether planted as avenues or in groups as groves and clumps.

The Institute of Field Archaeologists (IFA) has published a useful *Technical paper* on the applications of air photographs in planning archaeological work. This gives practical hints on how to plot features from air photographs and to use the results to plan an evaluation strategy. Such information is as useful for work on gardens and designed landscapes as any other type of site. The paper also gives details on how to commission new photographs (Palmer & Cox 1993).

Many early air photographs have now become historical records in their own right, demonstrating changes that have been made over the course of the 20th century. In the 1920s, the pioneering aerial archaeologist, O G S Crawford, flew over much of southern England taking photographs of historic sites. These often include gardens surrounding historic houses, and are useful records of these gardens before financial hardship of the 1930s caused many of them to become run down and, in some cases, to be abandoned. Thus a series of suspected Crawford photographs in the NMR show a garden area at Polesden Lacey, Surrey, planted by the last owner, Mrs Greville, in the early years of the 20th century that had been abandoned almost without trace by 1946 (Currie 2000a, 80, fig 6).

For all the literature on interpreting genuine archaeological features from the air, it is necessary to point out the problem of misidentifying geological features. These frequently show up as crop or parch marks. Wilson (2000, 163–209) gives a useful chapter on the types of geological and other non-archaeological features that can appear in air photographs. The misidentification of such features is not confined to the inexperienced. The author knows of numerous examples of experienced professionals, including himself, who have misidentified features seen from above. In fact, he would doubt there is a professional archaeologist in the world who has not been fooled at least once. The archaeological world is full of stories of wonderful howlers in this field, so pay careful attention to Wilson's chapter recommended above and treat air photographs with caution.

There are a number of places where the researcher can find air photographs. Most county Sites and Monuments Records (SMRs) hold relevant prints, and local record offices contain the occasional collection, but the larger collections can be found in the National Monuments Record, Kemble Drive, Swindon, Wilts, SN2 2GZ (tel 01793 414700; e-mail: nmrinfo@english-heritage.org.uk – for England), Royal Commission on the Ancient & Historic Monuments of Scotland, John Sinclair House, 16 Bernard Terrace, Edinburgh, EH8 9NX (tel 0131 662 1456; e-mail: postmaster@rcahms.gov.uk – for Scotland), Royal Commission on the Ancient & Historic Monuments of Wales, Crown Building, Plas Crug, Aberystwyth, Dyfed, SY23 1NJ (tel 01970 621233; e-mail: nmr.wales@rcahmw.org.uk – for Wales) and the Cambridge University Collection of Aerial Photographs, Mond Building, Free School Lane, Cambridge, CB2 3RF (tel 01223 334578; e-mail: aerial-photography@lists.cam.ac.uk). As stated above, most local authorities have commissioned aerial surveys of their district or county. Most counties have had at least three surveys carried out by now. Access is usually obtained by contacting the local authority for an appointment.

(See end of Section for notes)

Chapter 5: Archaeological survey methods

Field survey should be carried out before excavation whenever possible. It is a relatively simple matter to undertake, and has the advantage of being non-destructive and repeatable should the findings turn out to be controversial. There is little difference between surveying gardens and any other type of field monument.

In the past some garden historians and managers seem to have underestimated archaeological experience of landscape survey, and often turned to landscape architects for this sort of work. Phibbs' comment (1983, 169) that archaeologists have little experience of this sort of survey fails to take account of the extensive garden work undertaken by Christopher Taylor and the Royal Commission on the Historical Monuments of England (RCHME). This is evidenced by their respective publications *The Archaeology of Gardens* (1983), and the RCHME county volumes such as those for Dorset (vols. 2–5, 1970–75), Cambridgeshire (1968, 1972), and Northamptonshire (1975–82). It is reasonable to assert that these surveys are as good as anything I have seen from a non-archaeological surveyor. As well as these there were numerous garden surveys published by individual archaeologists before 1983; a few examples include Brown and Taylor (1972), Everson (1981) and Steane (1977), although the latter is more a synthesis of existing knowledge rather than true field survey.

Recognising the need for an initial survey at the earliest opportunity, it must be accepted that existing surface remains can often give a misleading impression of the development of a garden. This was admirably explained by Bond talking of moated sites, but it can be applied to field survey as a general method:

Archaeological field survey may be defined as the examination of sites on the ground without recourse to excavation. It is a reconnaissance technique rather than a means of producing final and definitive answers to all possible questions (Bond 1978, 14).

Taking account of these reservations, it has to be said that field survey of garden earthwork sites has advanced greatly in the last twenty years or so. It is not just that techniques have advanced, but interpretation is now beginning to become far more sophisticated. This is clearly the result of increased experience. One should bear in mind that it was less than thirty years ago when many garden earthworks were still being interpreted as deserted medieval villages (Taylor 1983, 8).

A good example of our more recent sophistication is the recognition of earthworks of medieval gardens, particularly those containing water features (Everson 1991, 9–12). Until the late 1980s any medieval earthworks that once held water were often automatically designated as fishponds, and although the keeping of fish may have been part of their purpose, such interpretation overlooked the ornamental aspect of these features almost entirely. During the 1980s there was still a lot of uncertainty in the minds of fieldworkers about the purpose of medieval ponds. As late as 1988 Christopher Taylor, considered to be one of the founding fathers of landscape and garden archaeology, could still be found writing:

'The sheer size and complexity of the resulting systems of ponds, channels and dams ... indicate that in many places the production of fish was on a scale which may have far exceeded the requirements of the owners.' (Taylor 1988, 467).

A few paragraphs on he states that '... there was... a major commercial basis to much of the production of fish throughout the high Middle Ages' (*ibid*, 468), something that has been vigorously disputed with regard to freshwater pond fish (Currie 1988a, 1989). In these works I argue that freshwater fish were a high status food reserved for the aristocracy through most of the medieval period, and commercial sale would have diluted this status. Although there were undoubtedly exceptions, the very size of many medieval fishpond complexes made them unsuitable solely as commercial propositions. Even though this author's works quoted above signalled a new look at medieval water features, it did not take the argument to its now obvious conclusion, and state that many of these large water complexes had significant ornamental aspects. It was only shortly after his 1988 statement that Taylor began to find cases where commercial explanations were untenable. In 1989 he published a paper on the medieval earthworks at Somersham Palace, suggesting the ponds were part of an ornamental design. Even here the reader can detect reservations that such a theory might be contested. The title of the paper 'Somersham Palace, Cambridgeshire: a medieval landscape for pleasure?' is qualified with a question mark (Taylor 1989).

Two years later Paul Everson, a colleague of Taylor's at the Royal Commission on the Historical Monuments of England, entitled a section in an essay on field survey as 'medieval water management as garden features' (Everson 1991, 9–12). Again the reader might detect some minor reservations, but, in general, that body (the RCHME) then most active in the field survey, seems to have advanced its view on large-scale medieval water features from being almost solely for commercial purposes to the point where it can be said that many of them had little commercial use at all, their purposes being largely to proclaim the status of the owner, and to ornament the landscape. Field survey by Everson and others has since identified many more sites where a previous utilitarian function has been replaced by one of ornamental or symbolic landscapes. More recent work has extended this to incorporate the reappraisal of many 16th- and 17th century sites, such as Wyeford Farm, Hampshire, where a site once thought to be a medieval moated site with fishponds has now been reinterpreted as an ornamental water 'garden' imbibed with symbolism that reflected the beliefs of its Puritan owner (Everson forthcoming).

The rapid change in interpretation of water features in the landscape is but one example of the way in which continuing field survey can aid our understanding of historic gardens and designed landscapes. This particular change in opinion had come about almost entirely through a reappraisal of topographical features supported by documentary research. Excavation played very little part in this work.

There can be little question that field survey can be undertaken more easily and quickly following the advances in technology that has brought electronic theodolites using satellites to obtain accurate location anywhere on the globe. Geographical Positioning Systems (GPS) have been a major advance in field survey, particularly as the equipment is now relatively inexpensive. A hand-held GPS, accurate to five metres in many circumstances, can be bought for £100. Such equipment is ideal for rapid survey of extensive sites, although it is not suitable for surveys where great accuracy is required. Nevertheless, GPS has made provisional survey extremely easy. All one has

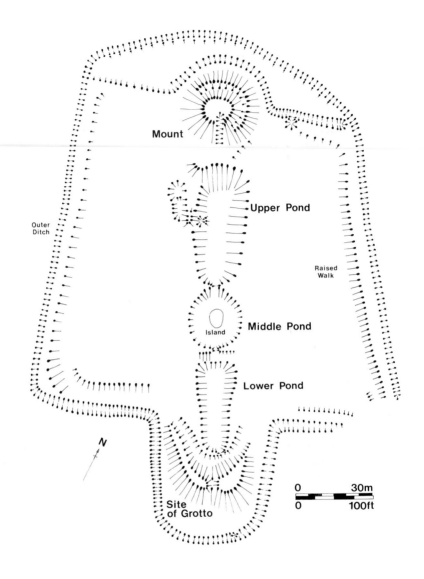

Mount

Outer
Ditch

Upper Pond

Raised
Walk

Island   Middle Pond

Lower Pond

N

Site
of Grotto

0		30m
0		100ft

*Figure 19: Earthwork survey of an unusual formal garden with possible Rococo
elements at Roxford, Hertfordbury, Herts. There are no references to this garden until
the mid-18th century, but it is assumed to be of early 18th-century date (for details
refer to Case Studies). This survey was undertaken by basic methods. Once a grid
had been set out using a manual theodolite, the earthworks were measured in using
tapes laid out in transects across the grid. See text for fuller explanation of method.*

to do is stand on the end of a linear earthwork, press a button and wait about thirty seconds, and a National Grid position is obtained. Depending on the regularity of the earthwork, one then goes to the other end and repeats the process. A rough plot of the earthwork alignment can then be transferred to a map. Accuracy is variable, depending on the weather, ground cover,[4] and position of satellites, but this author has managed accuracy to within a few metres in good conditions, although this can sometimes be ten metres or more in bad conditions.

Likewise the use of electronic theodolites has made accurate earthwork survey much simpler. Most practitioners use what are called 'Total Stations', an electronic theodolite that can measure distance and angle electronically, and which stores the data internally for transfer to a computer with the appropriate software. Advanced equipment incorporates GPS-capable technology, to locate the survey on the national grid. The system has the disadvantage of requiring two people to operate it. One stands with the theodolite, whilst another moves around the site as required with a reflective 'target', usually a small circular silver disc attached to a ranging rod or similar pole. Efficient coordination is usually obtained using radio equipment, or 'walky-talkies'. The theodolite operator is required to 'talk' the target-holder into position, and then direct a laser beam at the target. The information is then fed into the databank attached to the theodolite, and the next reading taken. The survey usually needs two or more fixed points of reference on which the final survey is based, but the laying out of a formalised grid, as is required for manual survey, is not generally required.

Although electronic equipment of this sort is 'relatively' inexpensive, the cost of a Total Station and the computer programmes necessary to plot out the surveys is usually around £10,000. Cheaper versions can be obtained around £5,000, but these have limitations. Consequently, such equipment may not be within the budget of smaller projects, and it is considered necessary within this handbook to give an overview of manual survey methods.

This author has carried out a number of earthwork surveys using a traditional manual theodolite, a few ranging rods, and some tapes. Although preferring to use the theodolite to lay out an accurate grid, this may not always be necessary, and ranging rods and tapes can still carry out worthwhile surveys, particularly those where information is needed quickly. Atkinson's *Field Archaeology* (1953) is still a useful text book outlining manual methods of surveying. It lists many variations on the simple ranging-rod-and-tape method that do not need to be repeated here.

It is proposed to detail the most useful form of manual earthwork survey in this volume. I intend to assume that a manual theodolite can be obtained to lay out the grid. Even in the most basic of surveys, a grid of some sort is essential for accuracy. The theodolite is set up first. This should be done at a convenient spot from which most of the site can be seen. This spot should be outside of the area to be surveyed. A quick scan through the telescope should be done to ensure that two lines at right angles can be set out from the machine that will encompass fully two sides of the survey area within the grid. This grid shall come to form a rectangle encompassing all the area proposed for survey. It is also important to try to lay out the grid along north–south and east–west lines. If possible try to get the outer grid lines to match up with the Ordnance Survey grid. The latter is not always essential, and there are often factors that prevent this, but tying in the grid with the Ordnance Survey map at a later date will be easier if your grid coincides with the national grid.

41

This is not always as easy as implied by some practitioners. Tying the grid in with a GPS system is by far the most reliable method, but cost keeps this out of the budget of the majority. Without a GPS system (a hand-held GPS metre is not accurate enough) one has to rely on taking points of reference off a feature on a large-scale OS map. This can be done reasonably accurately if there are buildings present, but even here the scale of the largest OS maps (1:2500) does not allow accuracy to more than 1m–2m. If there are no buildings present you will need to tie your grid into a field boundary or similar feature. However, OS field boundaries are often inaccurate. I have lost count of the number of times I have set up a grid based on OS field boundaries, only to find them highly inaccurate. This is often the result of a landowner resiting a boundary fence. The obvious answer here is to avoid boundaries marked only by wire fences if possible, but, unfortunately even a hedged boundary can be inaccurate. This is because most hedges are about 2m–3m thick (sometimes more), and it is not certain whether the OS surveyor has marked this from the far edge, the near edge or the centre. There are no set answers to this problem, and the surveyor often has to improvise. I have found liberal cursing to be most therapeutic whenever attempting to tie a survey grid into the national grid, with or without the use of GPS.

Once the theodolite is set up, and only then, position a stake centrally under the machine. Most machines have a viewer to allow this. Position the stake to line up with the central circle in the viewer, and, with the aid of a colleague, bang the stake firmly into the ground. Finally place a nail to the top of the stake, again positioned using the viewer. This is then used to fix tapes when measuring. It is essential to ensure the stake is very firm in the ground or the tension of the tape will pull it out of position. Firm stakes are also more resistant to cattle and other four-legged nuisances that can often co-habit with you on rural sites.

It needs to be stressed that you should set up the theodolite first, and then position your stake. Position the stake first, and then try to set the theodolite up over the centre of the peg at your peril! This can be done when you are very experienced, but it is not advised if you can avoid it.

Once this important first stake is in position, you are ready to lay out the rest of the grid. You should then send a colleague with a ranging rod to just beyond the far side of the site. Site him or her in using the theodolite, and replace the ranging rod with a stake. Again use the telescope to ensure the stake is in straight. If possible use a 100m tape and position the stake at a distance that is easy to remember. I try to set my grids up in units of 10m. For example the stake will be at 50m or 60m etc up to 100m depending on the size of the site. If you have to make a grid larger than 100m, set a stake at 100m, and then another beyond, using the same method as for the 100m mark. The first 100m tape will obscure the second tape, but apart from repositioning the theodolite (not recommended unless essential) you will have to improvise around the visual obstruction you have created.

Once the first line of the grid is laid out, set the angle reader on the theodolite at 0 degrees. Site it on to the far peg. Unclick the angle lock, and swing the telescope through 90 degrees. At this point lock the theodolite and repeat the process for the first line using your colleague with ranging rod. Again set the final peg on this line just beyond the limit of the area to be surveyed, and bang it into place guiding your colleague through the telescope to ensure the stake is straight. Getting the fourth stake into position to make a rectangular grid around your survey area is now relatively simple. We will presume that you were lucky enough to be able to encompass the site with a 100m square grid. All that is now required is to attach tapes to pegs 2 and 3 and pull them out until they intersect at 100m. At the point of intersection put in peg 4 and the rectangle is complete.

A survey can now be undertaken by measuring across the site from the grid. For example attach a 100m tape along the north side of the grid and a second along the south side. Take a third tape and place it at, say, 5m on the south tape and pull it out to 5m on the north tape. You can then move along the third tape measuring top and bottom of all earthworks and other features along that line and transferring them to a portable drawing board at a suitable scale.[5]

With regard to the measurement of earthworks, it needs to be stated that there is no exact position to determine 'top' and 'bottom' of a bank or similar feature. Given any five students, it is likely that all will have a slightly different interpretation of these points. This means that earthwork survey is not an exact science, like the survey of a building, where a wall has a definite point of contact with a tape. As long as the measurements are taken with a modicum of common sense and with a degree of consistency the survey can suffer discrepancies in interpretation of up to 50cm. After all, on an earthwork survey at 1:250 this is barely more than the thickness of a line. The earthworks should then been drawn using 'hachures', a tadpole shaped symbol that has the top of the bank at the thick end or 'head' and the bottom of the bank at the thin end or 'tail'.

The same grid can be used to produce a contour survey, giving a map of the relative heights across the site. This is done by taking height readings at regular intervals across the site (usually at 1m, 2m or 5m depending on the complexity of the topography). This should be tied into an OS bench mark so that the height above Ordnance Datum (sea level) can be calculated. Such surveys are particularly useful if the site contains water features, as the contours will invariably indicate the way water drained across the site. This is not always obvious from a hachure or topographical plan alone. The author's article on the suspected garden earthworks at the medieval hospital of St Cross, near Winchester, Hants displays plans of the site as both a hachured plan and as a contour survey (Currie 1998a).

Should the reader wish to learn other survey methods, they are referred to a manual on surveying. There are a number of good ones on the market (eg Hogg 1980). I have already referred to Atkinson (op cit), although this is rather out-of-date for more modern techniques, it is sufficient for most manual methods. Although out of print, it can be obtained through good second-hand bookshops or through a local library. Another useful low-cost method is to survey earthworks with a prismatic compass. This is a useful method for large areas, and lends itself especially to tree surveys (see below). Details of the methodology are given by Farrar (1987).

As well as measuring earthworks, there is one category of field survey appropriate to gardens and designed landscapes that is not normally carried out in other types of field archaeology, and that is a plant survey. This usually involves the plotting and identification of trees within the study area, although it can sometimes be extended to incorporate shrubs, particularly if they are considered to be part of historic plantings. It should be pointed out that tree surveys are frequently undertaken by landscape architects, and it is rare for archaeologists to undertake them personally. Nevertheless it is useful for archaeologists to be aware of the need for such surveys and to be able to carry them out if possible. The methods used are outlined in Phibbs (1983).

It is perhaps worth highlighting the uses of tree survey here, even if only in a cursory manner. Much useful information can be obtained about a site by walking around making a sketch plan of the tree placements. In particular the marked trees should be identified to species. From this sketch it is often possible to plot meaningful alignments. For example, a wood may have grown up over a garden site which includes lots of self-seeded saplings such as sycamore and ash. These are rarely planted as ornamentals in gardens. A sketch plan of the site eliminating trees that are obviously self-seeded could reveal alignments of yews or limes that could be the remnants of avenues or grown-out garden hedges. Should such an exercise seem to prove worthwhile it might then be time to consider a proper measured survey. In my own fieldwork I regularly add significant trees to my own measured surveys of earthworks, although, for full tree-by-tree surveys I tend to rely on the work of a landscape architect should one be employed on the project. There is, of course, no reason why archaeologists can not carry out their own tree surveys. Trees can be measured as easily as earthworks by a simple grid-based survey.[6]

There have been occasions when too much reliance has been placed on field survey alone. In many cases some theories derived from field survey need to be examined by excavation. The author's own work is no exception in this. The author's survey of the earthworks of the water garden at Southwick Park proved to be based on a simplistic interpretation, which needed to be re-analysed as a result of the excavation (Currie 1990a, 58). This was also the case at Castle Bromwich, where the initial survey by a landscape consultancy was found to have made unfounded assumptions on some points. As a result of these misinterpretations, excavation was undertaken on both sites trying to prove theories that turned out to be misguided.

The conclusions on survey suggests that they should be used with some caution. Certainly restoration plans should not be based on survey alone, without making some provision for an objective testing of the interpretation by excavation.

(See end of Section for notes)

Chapter 6: Historical building analysis

Buildings and built structures are often an integral part of any garden or designed landscape. In some cases the quickest and least destructive means of establishing a sequence of development in a garden is through the study of its surviving buildings. It can often be argued that it is the ornamental buildings that make the landscape. What is the overall importance of the buildings at sites like Stowe, Buckinghamshire, or Stourhead, Wiltshire? It is almost certain that without them both sites would not be such highly regarded garden designs.

Many gardens, such as Stowe and Stourhead, contain highly ornate garden buildings. Some are major monuments in their own right, but gardens contain numbers of more mundane structures that are often important to an understanding of the site's development. As well as containing elaborate temples, banqueting houses, eyecatchers, summer houses, grottoes, follies and mock ruins, they also contain less striking structures such as garden walls, greenhouses, aviaries and boiler houses. Even terraces often have revetment walls which can repay close study, and it is worth noting that statue bases are also built structures that may display useful information.

It is not intended here to give a full list of the type of structure likely to be encountered in gardens. A good summary of early garden building types can be found in Woodfield (1991), but this is not comprehensive. One only has to refer to Symes' *A glossary of garden history* (1993) to realise that the list is almost infinite. Whatever theme a designer has chosen, garden buildings are often made to fit in with this scheme. At Sir George Staunton's multi-theme designed landscape at Leigh Park, the exotic and esoteric buildings ornamenting the various parts of the garden included a Chinese Bridge, a mock fort, a cottage, a Corinthian bridge, a shell house, various pavilions, a 'Look-Out', a 'Green Arbour', a Cone House, a Swiss Cottage, a Turkish Tent, a Gothic Library, an Amazon Lily house, a *ferme ornée* and an obelisk, not to mention more mundane structures such as a walled garden with a crinkle-crankle wall, plus functional buildings such as greenhouses and potting sheds (Gladwyn 1991). Not all have survived, and some are only known from archaeological excavation, like the flint cill of a possible timber structure with a veranda overlooking the Dutch Garden (Currie 1995b).

Almost invariably the most important buildings, from the design point of view, were ornamental. These often did not have a deliberate function, although many became storehouses in the course of time. At Castle Bromwich Hall, opposing pavilions at either end of an axial walkway called the Holly Walk, were called the Orangery and the Music Room. The former was used as a greenhouse, where delicate shrubs such as orange trees were stored in movable pots. The Music Room was used as a place where musical instruments were kept (Currie & Locock 1993a). However, both features were mainly ornamental, and their functions could have been performed more satisfactorily elsewhere. Very few of the structures at Leigh Park had any real function other than to ornament the landscape, although a tenant may have lived in the 'cottage' to add to its authenticity. For a while, William Beckford of Fonthill Abbey, Wiltshire, kept a permanent hermit in his garden hermitage.

*Figure 20: Lyveden New Bield, Northants: the late 16th-century T-Shaped
Banqueting House symbolising the Holy Trinity.*

Historic building recording and analysis is a technique used by other disciplines as well as archaeology. Historic building specialists used to be largely recruited from architectural historians and architects who had taken a special interest in historic buildings. There can be no questioning the value of the contributions of such people, but their methods tend to be based more on a description of the architectural style of a building rather than a systematic recording, which is the more general method of the archaeologist. The difference in approach tends to come from the archaeological tradition of total recording that is born out of the archaeologist's experience of working on structures that are due for destruction. In more recent years a series of levels of recording has evolved, based largely on the RCHME's *Historic Building Recording. A Descriptive Specification* (RCHME 1991).

This useful system breaks building recording down into four levels, graded according to the importance of the building and the extent of the damage likely to be caused to it. It is common for buildings to be recorded because they are going to be altered or destroyed, although some more research-based projects may simply be recording them to obtain information about a site.

The quickest and simplest method of recording a building is by photographic survey. Coupled with a written description this can provide the basic data necessary to begin an analysis of the structure. Where funds are available it is useful to make a measured survey. This will include the elevations of the structure and a plan of the various floor levels. It is rare for garden buildings to comprise more than two storeys, so the plans are seldom of the same complexity as some dwelling houses. When drawing elevations, the recorder should take care to note any changes in materials or surfacings. Even when a building is built entirely of brick it is possible to notice

Figure 21: Hanbury Hall, Worcester: a fine example of an early 18th-century orangery

repairs, blocking of windows and doors, and extensions through changes in the colour of the brickwork, straight joints and even differences in the mortar used.

There are a number of publications that give details of some of the more advanced methods of building recording. A useful booklet for beginners in structural recording is the Rescue booklet by Barbara Hutton, *Recording standing buildings* (1986). This volume is simplicity itself to understand, and once absorbed will help even the most inexperienced recorders to make useful surveys. This book deals mainly with vernacular dwelling houses, but it is easy to convert the methods to garden buildings. Two booklets from this present series of *Practical Handbooks* are invaluable during building recording, and should be kept in the recording bag when on site. These are Alcock *et al*, *Recording timber-framed buildings: an illustrated glossary* (1996) and Alcock & Hall, *Fixtures and fittings in dated houses 1567–1763* (1994). Many readers will note that timber-framed buildings tend to be rare in gardens, and think the former might be of limited value. This is true, but most garden structures have roofs made of timber, and a glossary of terms is a useful book to have at hand. In the case of the fixtures and fittings booklet I find this invaluable for helping to date buildings. Until I had this book the usefulness of features common to most garden building such as door hinges and window catches in dating buildings had not seriously occurred to me.

The Association of Archaeological Illustrators & Surveyors has published a booklet with the misleading title, *The survey and recording of historic buildings* (Andrews *et al* 1995), but the reader should be warned that this book only deals with the most advanced forms of building survey. In this case only subjects of photogrammetry, rectified photography, the use of CAD and EDM *without reflectors*, and the use of digital data in building recording are covered. Such a publication is useful for

47

Figure 22: The Grange, Northington: one of the best neo-classical garden buildings in the UK; originally built as an orangery, it was later converted into a conservatory. It has recently been converted into an opera house, for which it won an RIBA award.

experienced building recorders who wish to expand their knowledge, and it is unfortunate that the title implies a more general handbook.

As implied above, gardens are likely to contain all sorts of whimsical buildings and structures. Learning to identify the different types only comes with experience. An example of the difficulty in recognising the purpose of such structures occurred in 1992 when the author was asked to undertake some recording work on a partly sunken garden structure that had formerly been part of Milnthorpe House, a mid-19th-century suburban villa then on the outskirts of Winchester (Hants). The structure had already been the subject of a published archaeological note that concluded that it was a possible ice house (Morris 1987). The owners, Mr & Mrs Chapman, had subsequent doubts about this interpretation, and the author was called in to record the building ahead of renovation. This feature was a rectangular brick structure 3.8m by 3.2m, with a vaulted top and a crude broken pediment surmounting the north face. It was partly sunk into a mound that was itself part of a series of terraced walks cut into a steep chalk hillside. Clearance by the owner revealed a metal pipe protruding from the bottom of the north face and the top of the west face. Inside was a floor of thick perforated slates sufficient to take a man's weight, with a shallow void beneath. On top of the slates there had been a layer of course flint chippings, but these had been removed by the owner, who had mistaken them as an accumulation of debris. The interior was entered by a circular hole in the apex of the vault only 0.45m wide, making access for an adult male difficult. The site had been recently visited by a recognised ice house specialist who had expressed doubt on the earlier interpretation, and this led the owner to contact the author in the hope of obtaining an explanation.

Work on the site comprised a measured survey of the terraces to put the structure in context. It was noted that from the top of the structure, an exceptional view of the west front of Winchester Cathedral could be obtained. There was further tentative evidence of yew planting on the terraces with gaps so that the view of the cathedral was not interrupted. From this it was concluded that the structure, which was clearly utilitarian, also fulfilled some decorative function within the garden. This was supported by evidence for a ruinous flint and brick wall at the base of the mound, which gave the feature a pleasing appearance when viewed from the north.

Some earth was removed from around the sides of the structure, but apart from revealing the metal pipes this gave no further clue regarding the purpose of the structure. The pipes suggested that water entered the building from the top and left it from the base of the mound. An OS map dated 1869 marked a structure on or near the present site as 'well house', but the previous recorder of the building had considered this to be a 'misinterpretation' (Morris 1987, 258–60). The map did not appear to be particularly accurate, and later changes in boundaries had made it difficult to tell if this 'well house' was on the same location as the structure. Taking the view that the building was some form of 'well', the author carried out research on water supply in suburban villa gardens. Knowing that J C Loudon's *The suburban gardener and villa companion* (1838) was probably the best source for such information, it was discovered 'Every dwelling house requires a supply of water... [that] may be collected... in tanks and cisterns...where it is desirable to keep the water cool, the tank should be sunk so deep, as to be beyond the influence of the sun' (Loudon 1838, 741).

Although it had become clear that the structure was a tank for collecting water, the perforated slates and coarse materials on them still did not make sense until reference to Singer *et al*'s, *A history of technology* made it clear the coarse material was an early form of water purifier known as the 'slow sand filter' (*ibid*, iv, 499) still used by water companies around the world today. Finally after five years of pondering by local archaeologists, the structure was discovered to be a small water purifying reservoir for Milnthorpe House. Thus what was the latest technology of its day had been incorporated into the terraced garden design to appear as an ornamental feature (Currie 1997b). A similar type of concealment can be seen at Lytes Cary, Somerset, where what appears to be a circular medieval dovecote is a water tower in disguise (James Bond pers comm).

The unusual nature of garden structures is further emphasised by other publications of this author that have included the recording and/or analysis of above ground structures. To date this has involved the recording of a grotto, an antiquarian ruin, and two cascades, one associated with the remains of two grottoes. All are dealt with as case studies in this book. However, it ought to be stressed that strictly a cascade is an upstanding structure. Both cascades at The Gnoll and Upper Lodge, Bushy Park (see case studies) contained considerable upstanding structure that were recorded in the same manner as one would approach a standing wall. The majority of the remains at Upper Lodge were attached to a revetment wall.

Martin Locock's (1990a, 1990b) papers on the structural remains at Castle Bromwich give an idea of the sort of results such survey can produce in qualified hands. Here it was decided to examine the documentary records for brick making on the site in the first half of the 18th century and to compare it with the standing garden walls. These were quite considerable as a programme of extending the garden between 1730 and 1747 involved the enclosure of a further 3.5 hectares of garden behind brick walls. The records showed that the brick making was conducted on a seasonal basis by local estate workers and tenants as their annual cycle allowed. In this case, brick making was undertaken in the autumn after the harvest had been brought in. The brick-makers used temporary kilns, firing the produce on site or nearby in batches of 1300. What was remarkable in this process was that they were marking their bricks. Each hundredth brick was tally-marked in a degenerate form of Roman numerals. Examination of the walls themselves showed these marks on the faces of the bricks. Obviously some of the tally marks were invisible when the marked face was set inwards, but enough were visible to confirm that the bricks were, indeed, made in batches of 1300 as stated in the estate records: no tally marks beyond the number thirteen being encountered (Locock 1990a). The fact that the tally marks occurred primarily in the extended garden helped confirm that the bricks were used in these new walls, a matter that was contentious at the time of the study, but was subsequently confirmed by further documentary research (Currie & Locock 1993a, 196–97n).

The detailed study of the garden walls enabled a number of revealing conclusions to be drawn. At the time these ideas seemed impossible to certain members of the garden management committee. Amongst the conclusions drawn from the work of combined structural analysis and documentary research was that the seasonal nature of the work had a clear effect on the progress of the garden development. Not only were the brick-makers only producing for a limited time each year, the work of construction was being funded from the annual revenue of the estate (Locock 1993d, 166). This resulted in the otherwise inexplicable long time-scale for constructing this large walled garden,

Figure 23: Castle Bromwich Hall, West Midlands: close up of 18th-century garden wall showing inscribed tally mark. Here four lines depict a corrupt form of the Roman numeral IV. (Photo by Martin Locock)

which continued roughly from 1733 through to 1746, the year before the owner, John Bridgeman's death. This work included putting up the two summer houses that were incorporated within the line of the wall. Some interesting points about the garden walls were that they were built following the slope of the land, not to a level line as in modern practice. The foundations were also incredibly shallow considering the sandy nature of the local soils, being barely two bricks deep in most places. This resulted in the walls, which were 2m high, needing support. In the 19th century brick buttresses had to be added where the walls were weakest. When the lower garden was eventually abandoned after 1936, considerable lengths of the wall fell down and had to be rebuilt in the 1980s when the gardens were restored.

The brick-makers of Castle Bromwich made approximately four million bricks as part of their seasonal occupation during the period 1730–47. These bricks included specialist bricks such as coping bricks and u-shaped drainage bricks. Although they could be seen as part of the wider Yardley industry in the Forest of Arden, they seem to have developed their own local techniques. It is surprising that tally-marked bricks could not been found at other garden sites. Only one other garden has been found to exhibit this characteristic, and that was an isolated incident of a small number of marked bricks found in the garden wall at Packwood House in neighbouring Warwickshire (*ibid*).[7]

Locock's (*op cit*) work on the garden walls at Castle Bromwich demonstrated what can be done from a study of the most basic structural element of historic gardens, the garden wall.

The work at Castle Bromwich also included a study of the garden nails left in the walls from years of training espalier fruit trees and other plants against them. It was

Figure 24: The Dean's House, Wimborne Minster, Dorset: a crinkle-cranckle brick wall, the alcoves forming extra protection for delicate fruit trees trained against the wall.

51

noted that such a study could be used to try to identify phases of planting along such walls. At Shaw House, Berkshire, preliminary observations identified three phases of nails attached to one length of garden wall (Currie 1998b, 72–73). There is clear scope to obtain far more information from the humble garden wall than has previously been recognised.

(See end of Section for notes)

Chapter 7: Geophysical survey

By Martin Locock

The issue of whether to use geoprospective techniques on garden sites, and if so, which to adopt, has been the subject of considerable debate. A pragmatic view, from an archaeologist's standpoint, that many surveys are ineffective or unhelpful (for example Currie & Locock 1991; 1992) can be set against arguments and case-studies in favour of their wide use (Aspinall & Pocock 1995; Cole *et al* 1997).

By the late 1980s, geophysical techniques had become established in the suite of investigative methods for examining sites; within a research-driven philosophy, application of the precautionary principle resulted in the use of relatively rapid and inexpensive non-destructive survey techniques as a prelude to conventional excavation. In such a context, the issue of the reliability of the surveys, and the accuracy of their interpretations, was not considered critical, since they were perceived as an additional strand of investigation. With the shift towards developer funding following the issuing of Planning Policy Guidance no 16 (PPG16), and its associated framework of 'reasonableness', evaluation, and specified approved methodologies, this ceased to be the case: resources expended on Method A would not be available for Method B; and if Method A produced no indication of surviving deposits, there would be no follow-up phase.

The Leverhulme Research Project framed the question for gardens thus: 'Which techniques produce results which are a useful guide to an exploration strategy?', and commissioned a range of surveys on the test site at Castle Bromwich Hall. The surveys were undertaken by Bradford University in 1989, and were compared against the subsequent excavated evidence (Currie & Locock 1991). As a result, the Leverhulme team concluded that the results were unhelpful: important buried remains had not been located, while some anomalies proved to have no stratigraphic correlation. Aspinall and Pocock (1995), in their review of geophysics on garden sites, commented on the Castle Bromwich Hall results, using further filtering to resolve the surveys into what are interpreted as previous layouts of the Best Garden and Middle Terrace. Although these are credible as possible layouts, extensive excavations (published in Currie and Locock 1993) failed to confirm their existence.

Regardless of the *minutiae* of individual cases, there is a clear division in the literature between those who argue that geophysics should be used as a matter of course, and those that are much more doubtful. There is broad agreement about the types of target which can be identified (see Table). The two sides are in fact saying complementary things: the 'pro-geophysics' side say that geophysical survey can successfully locate garden *structures*, while the doubters say that it cannot reliably locate garden *features*. If testing for the presence of a building, wall or drain is critical to the restoration design of a garden, then clearly geophysics has a role. If the question is the broader one, of where the soft features are best preserved or most complex, then it may not provide useful answers. The ICOMOS UK *Guidelines for the use of Archaeology in Gardens, Parks and Estates* (1998) identify the role of geophysical survey as allowing:

investigation of buried **structural elements** of the garden or landscape not normally detectable at the surface without physical intervention (emphasis added).

TABLE 7.1: Geophysical identification of garden features

Walls and buildings	Good
Culverts and drains	Fair to good
Large "soft" features (beds)	Fair to poor
Gravel paths	Fair to poor
Small cut features (planting holes)	Poor

A recurrent issue on garden sites is the nature of present vegetation; in particular, the presence of root systems of mature trees often masks any anomalies over a considerable area (Clark 1990; Gaffney *et al* 1991). Another is the resolution that can be expected; in general, features smaller than 1m diameter are unlikely to be located since a single 'spike' reading would be dismissed; Cole *et al* (1997) note the successful location of tree-planting holes at Barrow Hills, Radley, Oxfordshire, by magnetometry, but, in this case, the features were 2–3m in diameter.

In looking at the effectiveness of specific techniques, the lack of confirmatory data is a major obstacle. Aspinall and Pocock (1995) present five detailed case-studies, of which only one (Castle Bromwich Hall) had been tested by excavation. Similarly, of the 31 other sites cited by Cole *et al* (1997), only two, Kirby Hall (Northants), and Barrow Hills, Radley, Oxfordshire, were excavated. In other cases, the success of the survey has been assessed on the grounds of agreement with old paintings or garden designs, or internal likelihood. To this small number can be added Tredegar House (Newport), Aberglasney (Carmarthenshire), and Hanbury Hall (Worcestershire).

The results of Castle Bromwich Hall can be briefly summarised as showing that neither earth resistance nor magnetometry proved effective at locating what the excavators considered to be 'target' features; reprocessing of the resistivity data achieved some improvement, although some of the features identified in this re-interpretation proved on excavation not to exist. Magnetometry successfully identified a set of iron pegs which formed part of the early 20th-century garden layout, supporting trellis arches, but no other features.

At Tredegar House, Newport, a resistivity survey of an extensive area was undertaken, followed by excavation and restoration of the Orangery Garden (Ewart 1990). The survey had been interpreted as showing an 18th-century formal layout of paths and beds. Excavation showed that the features corresponding to the survey were more recent drainage features immediately beneath the surface; the 18th-century ground surface lay below this, masked from the survey.

At Aberglasney, resistivity survey of the Cloister Garden identified eight features (Briggs 1999, fig. 11), including a culvert, paths, cobbled areas, trees and possible beds. Comparison of the interpretation with the results of total excavation (Blockley & Halfpenney 2002) reveals that only the culvert and two features shown on 1880 Ordnance Survey maps were correctly located. At Hanbury Hall, Worcestershire, (Currie 1996a) resistivity survey in advance of machine clearance and excavation

Figure 25: Castle Bromwich Hall, West Midlands: resistivity being undertaken in the Best Garden.

identified a pattern of linear features; on excavation these proved to be a post-medieval drainage system, again overlying the garden levels.

Thus of the mainstream techniques, resistivity has the best track record, with the important caution that apparently-convincing layouts that such surveys reveal may be shown by excavation to be misleading. The higher precision technique of Ground Penetrating Radar has been little used to date; the costs and problems with vegetation cover make it problematic, although it has been tried with success elsewhere (Conyers, in press).

A final option often recommended in garden contexts is dowsing. Many archaeologists have adopted the stance that dowsing cannot work and therefore have given it little credence. The Leverhulme project, in response to anecdotal evidence for its success, undertook a test to examine whether it worked in practice (Locock 1995), and concluded that it largely did not. In a review of the broader application of dowsing to archaeology, van Leusen (1999) notes that the reported results of the Leverhulme exercise were distorted in favour of dowsing by the scoring system adopted. This experience is echoed by Jacques' experience at Chiswick, where some results were shown to be 'moderately correct' by excavation, but some were not. He cautions that 'the main practitioner ... goes much too far in his interpretations of his own reactions' (Jacques 1992, 20).

Since the Castle Bromwich tests further resistivity work has been undertaken on garden sites such as Wilton House, Wiltshire; Kirby, Northamptonshire; and Hanbury Hall, Worcestershire. At the two former sites, it has been claimed that resistivity was successful in locating buried features associated with the garden. However, at Kirby this success seems to be largely restricted to the location of structural features, often of some size. Although a resistivity plot of the Wilton data seems to match up reasonably well with views of the garden made in 1654 (Cole *et al* 1997, 28), there are anomalies, and the results are not known to have been tested by excavation. The author has not seen conclusive evidence that these surveys were able to locate plant beds, or other plant related features. These features are crucial to the identification of the internal design of the garden, and are just as important to garden historians as structural features. Although, it is undoubtedly of help to be able to locate structures in gardens, to be of essential use, a prospecting method must be able to demonstrate its ability to locate features related specifically to horticultural activity.

It was possible to test the results of the survey undertaken at Hanbury Hall by excavation under the direction of the same team that did the initial tests at Castle Bromwich. Here the site was entirely under grass, and comprised stratigraphy far less complex than that at Castle Bromwich. Also the situation was not confused by the massive terrace dumps that were found at Castle Bromwich. For the most part, the *parterre* design at Hanbury was laid directly into the undisturbed local clays, and, apart from alterations to the edges of the garden, the internal design was left largely undisturbed until the site was grassed over in the later eighteenth century. Factors not aiding the interpretation of the resistivity survey such as root disturbance, massive soil dumping, and a complex sequence of designs overlying one another were not present over much of the Hanbury site, as they had been at Castle Bromwich.

Nevertheless, the Hanbury survey was unhelpful to the archaeologists. The survey failed to locate any garden features of relevance, picking up only surface tile land drains of relatively recent date. It consistently failed to locate any features deeper than 0.25m, despite the testing interval of one metre. Well-defined plant beds, up to 0.5m deep, cut into a compact red clay, and filled with a loose loam, were consistently missed by the survey, as was a massive structural feature (a large gate pier), less than 0.5m beneath the surface, and brick revetment walls at 0.35m depth. If anything, the survey acted negatively in that it wasted much time and resources because the excavators found themselves forced to excavate the surface land drains located to eliminate them as significant features.

On the positive side, a magnetometer survey at Bantock Park, West Midlands, produced reasonably good results on a late Victorian and Edwardian garden being restored by Wolverhampton Metropolitan Borough Council. Here paths dividing a small *parterre* were located with some accuracy, although it might be stressed that these remains, being relatively recent, existed immediately beneath the turf at a depth of less than 0.2m (Ponsford 2000, 306).

The conclusions have to be that geophysics should be used with caution on most garden sites. Both on sandy and clay soils, resistivity has often been found to be wanting. It is not sufficient to claim success from the results of work where the only significant features located are structural. The results at Hanbury have demonstrated that even this ability is not consistent, and until a methodology is devised that can consistently identify plant beds, the method has restricted uses in garden work. This is view is largely accepted by protagonists of the method. Cole *et al* (1997, 38) state, '...[the] long-term potential of geophysical prospecting to garden archaeology is still difficult to assess'.

These authors claim geophysical techniques are at their 'most proficient' at detecting masonry structures, a view held by this writer. However, the view that 'more subtle traces' such as flower beds and tree pits can be detected has only been shown in exceptional circumstances. They also admit that geophysics is 'vulnerable' on sites where there is superimposition of features from later phases (*ibid*).

Nevertheless, with the increasing need to preserve archaeology *in situ*, and the constraints of a limited budget, it is still desirable to undertake a survey prior to any ground disturbance. However, no important decisions should be made on the basis of geophysics alone, and some attempt, no matter how small, should be made to test the interpretation, as the lesson of Hanbury clearly demonstrated.

(See end of Section for notes)

Chapter 8: Excavation techniques

GENERAL CONSIDERATIONS: AREA EXCAVATION OR TEST TRENCHING?

This chapter need not attempt a detailed description of how to excavate a site. There are many good books on that subject to which the reader should refer (eg Barker 1982; Roskams 2001). The purpose of this chapter is try to inform the reader how gardens might differ from more general archaeological sites, and what is the best way to excavate them effectively.

Many manuals on archaeology tend to assume that the area to be excavated will be of a reasonable size so that area excavation can be used. The reality is that most garden excavations are undertaken on limited budgets with very restricted aims. It is rare that an archaeologist will be invited to carry out the total excavation of a garden. There is even a strong argument that would indicate that this is not necessarily a good thing. Today archaeology is as much about conserving the past as destroying it, and excavation is a destructive process. There have been instances in the not too distant past when gardens were excavated without the same sort of care that might have been lavished on more mainstream sites, like a prehistoric henge or medieval abbey. If the work is not going to be done to the highest standard possible, it is preferable not to excavate at all. The small scale excavations that are favoured today are less destructive of archaeology than large-scale area or total excavation.

Two examples of a less than satisfactory situation regarding garden excavation can be cited. In the 1930s George Chettle carried out a large-scale excavation of the garden at Kirby Hall, Northamptonshire (see Fig 1), following the monument being taken into national guardianship. It is uncertain exactly how effective this excavation was, but its purpose was to recreate the plan of a period garden that could be planted on the site to enhance the visitor's perception of the building's environment. In the 1980s English Heritage decided that the 1930s recreation was likely to have been crude, considering the standards of the time. As a consequence they decided to attempt a more accurate 'restoration' of the site. The new excavations concluded that while the old excavations had 'been shown ... to reflect, faithfully in part, a former layout of the garden, they were anachronistic...' (Dix *et al* 1995, 299). That is, the restored garden did not match the late 17th-century date that English Heritage wanted. These levels had been removed in the 1930s, making it impossible to know what the garden looked like at that time. The result was that the newer restoration had to 'look to other sites for appropriate designs' (*ibid*). Hence, the 'total' excavation of the garden in the 1930s resulted in problems in the 1980s.

The second example is the total excavation of the Privy Garden at Hampton Court. Here the archaeologists were instructed to wipe 'the slate clean by stripping the whole two hectares of the site' (Thurley 1995, 9). The platte bandes, that is the archaeological features that made up the plant beds, 'once they had been identified by hand, were dug out mechanically' (*ibid*, caption to plate 17, p. 13). If future heritage managers wish to revisit the archaeology at Hampton Court, the situation at Kirby will be repeated because the evidence has been removed. It is not considered that the

Figure 26: Castle Bromwich Hall, West Midlands: linear plant beds clearly shown as dark lines against the reddish sandy soils of the Midlands

archaeologists can be blamed for either situation as they were merely doing what the site managers instructed, but one feels that it might have been better if total excavation had not been undertaken on either site.

The moral of this tale is that large-scale area excavation (particularly total excavation) should be resisted on garden sites unless the site is likely to be destroyed by development. Then the ethical rule of 'preservation by record' can apply. The message that seemed to emanate from the Privy Garden at Hampton Court, which was a Scheduled Ancient Monument and part of a World Heritage Site, was that standards of practice which exist for other archaeological sites can be disregarded on garden sites. Somehow the idea has arisen in certain quarters that gardens are not 'proper' archaeology, an attitude that needs to be discouraged.

Although concerns have been expressed about the use of archaeology in garden restoration, and about the very ethics of restoration, particularly single period examples (Currie & Locock 1992; Currie & Scholtz 1996), it is encouraging to find that Brian Dix, the excavation director at Hampton Court, has similar misgivings about the misuse of the discipline, particularly on sites where the evidence may not be clear cut.

The limitations of surviving physical evidence have to be appreciated and inter-pretation that cannot be sustained must be avoided, however frustrating this might be to the client … restorers should beware of prejudging findings: a judgement based purely on archival sources of what is important at a site may find itself in conflict with subsequent archaeological evidence (Dix 1997, 13)

Figure 27: Hanbury Hall, Worcester: more linear plant beds just below the surface being excavated by Dr Andrew Reynolds, now of University College, London. This time the beds survive in heavy clay (cf Castle Bromwich)

The approximate same view expressed by Currie and Locock (1992) about garden managers being tempted to manipulate archaeological evidence if it did not suit their pre-ordained restoration plan five years earlier had caused an uproar amongst traditionalists in the garden history world (*cf* letters following the 1992 article). Just as garden archaeology itself has advanced rapidly since the late 1980s, it is hoped that attitudes towards restoration have matured in the garden history world generally.

In discussing the excavation of gardens the prevailing situation of the day needs to be considered. Since the introduction of PPG16 in November 1990 (Department of the Environment 1990), a large number of archaeological interventions on garden sites have been the result of proposed development and their attendant planning conditions. Excavation is still undertaken to inform restoration and site management, particularly on sites managed by Trusts. The National Trust regularly conducts largely small-scale explorations on its many garden sites, as do private trusts and English Heritage on its guardianship monuments, but in general large-scale excavation is something that is done less and less. It is therefore considered that in order to be able to understand excavation on garden sites, the reader needs to be aware of how to undertake 'evaluations' and 'watching briefs', presently the most common forms of intervention.

The Institute of Field Archaeologists divides archaeological 'excavation' into three stages of decreasing importance: 'excavation', 'evaluation' and 'watching brief'. A summary of their definitions are as follows:

1. Excavation: archaeological excavation is a programme of controlled, intrusive fieldwork with defined research objectives which examines, records and interprets archaeological deposits, features and structures and, as appropriate, retrieves artefacts, ecofacts and other remains within a specific area or site. The records made and objects gathered during fieldwork are studied and the results of that study published in detail appropriate to the project design.

2. Evaluation: a limited programme of intrusive fieldwork (mainly test-trenching) which determines the presence or absence of archaeological features, structures, deposits, artefacts or ecofacts within a specified land unit or area. If they are present, this will define their character, extent, and relative quality, and allow an assessment of their worth in local, regional and national terms.

3. Watching brief: a formal programme of observation and investigation conducted during any operation carried out for non-archaeological reasons. This will be within a specific area or site ... where there is a possibility that archaeological deposits may be disturbed or destroyed. The programme will result in the preparation of a report and ordered archive.

During the Leverhulme Project at Castle Bromwich Hall an attempt was made to assess the most effective way to excavate a garden. It was suggested that on projects with a limited budget sample trenches were often preferred in gardens to area excavation, where a large area is completely stripped (Currie & Locock 1991a, 79–80). An exception to this could be when a specific feature needs to be stripped entirely, as the West Pond at Castle Bromwich, but even here test trenches were excavated first to

Figure 28: Castle Bromwich Hall, West Midlands: test trenching writ large. A 50m long test trench across the Best Garden. A young Dr Dan Hicks, now of Bristol University and an avid promoter of historical archaeology, discusses the archaeology with Heidi Taylor in the foreground.

indicate the type of survival likely to be encountered (Currie 1990b). As well as keeping disturbance of the garden to a minimum, the former method works on the theory that the layout of many gardens contains a form of symmetry. This means that features found in one part of the garden are often mirrored in another. This is generally true of most historic gardens from the Roman period onwards, although it is recognised that gardens of the landscape movement do not have this tendency.

This method has advantages not only for the gardener and the archaeologist, but enables large areas of the site to be preserved untouched for future generations. This is a most important consideration as archaeology is a non-repeatable exercise, and preservation enables controversial results to be checked when techniques have improved in the future.

This does not mean that area excavation should be dismissed entirely. Limited area excavation, used in conjunction with test trenching proved particularly effective in the Best Garden at Castle Bromwich. However, financial constrains may exclude area excavation as test trenching is by far the most effective method when the budget is limited. For larger projects area excavation used in conjunction with test trenching should prove the most effective technique. In the Best Garden at Castle Bromwich excavation of about 5% of the garden was enough to get a good idea of the previous designs. Although some questions still remain to be answered fully, by careful siting of trenches, it was possible to recover most of the information required. Previous garden designs could probably be determined by excavating 20% or less on any given site.

DEVISING A METHODOLOGY FOR GARDEN SITES

The first thing that needs to be undertaken, whatever the form of investigation, is to set out a site grid. The method for doing so is described in the chapter on survey (see above). The excavator should ensure that the entire site is included within the grid. If, for some reason it cannot, perhaps because garden walls inhibit the positioning of the grid pegs, the excavator should make the grid as large as possible in the circumstances, and allocate grid co-ordinates that allow the grid to be expanded if required. In every case the grid peg in the SW corner of the grid defines the co-ordinates of the rest of the grid. The co-ordinates should be allocated as on an OS map using 'eastings' and 'northings'. Do not, unless you are absolutely certain that the grid will not need enlarging later, make the SW grid peg 0/0. Instead make it 100/100 or a reading that will allow for expansion. In the case of 100/100, this gives the excavator the opportunity to expand the grid 100m to both south and west if required. Setting out a proper site grid will enable all the trenches excavated to be accurately plotted into the site plan, and on to the national grid, regardless of the type of intervention proposed. Admittedly it is sometimes awkward to lay a grid out for a watching brief, especially on busy building sites, but the archaeologist should always consider doing so if it is possible. Excavation and evaluation should always be based on a site grid.

Even if you have sufficient funding and manpower to carry out a full-scale excavation on a garden site, it is highly recommended that you carry out an evaluation before commencing the main phase of work. This will allow you to judge if the survival of archaeological stratigraphy is sufficient to make the full-scale excavation worthwhile. There is nothing worse than making costly and time-consuming preparations for excavation only to find that the expected archaeology has been largely removed.

Figure 29: Leigh Park (Hants): a perfectly preserved garden path surviving just below later turf. Note the gravel is rolled in with its clay matrix in a cambered form to allow water to drain off freely.

In the case of formal gardens a decent evaluation is often sufficient to obtain enough information to achieve the research aims on its own. Bearing in mind that most planning authority archaeological curators working under PPG16 require a minimum of 5% of the site to be evaluated, and the latest English Heritage guidelines have suggested 15%, such areas were as much as were excavated during the research excavations at Castle Bromwich, the site generally considered to be one of the benchmarks for British garden archaeological practice.

The reader should consider that evaluations are invariably undertaken using machinery these days. This author still carries out a percentage of his evaluations by hand when the circumstances require. The author's evaluations at Leigh Park, Hampshire, The Wakes, Hampshire, and Hanbury Hall, Worcestershire were all carried out by hand without any recourse to machinery (Currie 1995b, 1995c, 1996a). However, there can be no question that the archaeological world's attitude to the use of machinery has changed since these projects were carried out. In 1999 the author undertook an evaluation using machinery at The Workhouse, Southwell, potentially a most unpromising site, but the results were possibly as good as could have been expected from hand excavation (Currie 1999).

The conclusion to be drawn from this is that in an ideal world all excavation should be undertaken entirely by hand, but the careful use of machinery is now acceptable for evaluation. The specifications issued by most planning archaeologists limit the use of machinery, even in evaluation, to the removal of topsoil and overburden. Machines are not allowed to be used in the excavation of features. This needs to be done by hand, as soon as they are identified. A typical planning authority specification on the use of machinery usually reads something like this:

Trenches may be excavated initially by machine, but these must be fitted with a toothless ditching bucket and must only be used to remove topsoil and over-burden down to the top of the first significant archaeological deposit or to the top of undisturbed geological deposits, whichever is encountered first. Once the first significant archaeological horizon is reached, all excavation should be by hand. All machining should be undertaken under the supervision of a qualified archaeologist.

These standard requirements tend to be a bit ambiguous when applied to garden sites. What is usually considered 'overburden' on many garden sites can often be significant garden horizons. At the Southwell Workhouse, linear features that turned out to be plant beds were barely 100mm below the surface in places (*ibid*). Likewise plant beds at Castle Bromwich were encountered regularly within 200mm of the surface. In the Rose Garden, where a set of linear planting beds were preserved, this was barely 150mm below the present ground surface, despite the site having been cultivated using machinery within the previous year (see Fig 28). Even more remarkable was the slanting angle of these beds when seen in section, which clearly showed the consistent side from which the gardener dug each trench (*cf* Currie & Locock 1993a, 125, Fig. 8, section b–b). The lesson to be taken from these examples is that machines should be used with the greatest care on garden sites or important evidence may be lost.

If the area being excavated is suspected of having contained plant beds in historic times then machining should be limited to the top 100–150mm in the first instance. The trench should then be trowelled back and cleaned by hand to look for signs of cultivation. The later often occurs as linear features, particularly in areas used to grow vegetables. Some varieties of flowers and shrubs, such as box edging, also tend to be planted in lines. Within the more important ornamental areas of the garden, plant beds can take on all sorts of random or geometric shapes. Again they can occur very close to the surface, as in the Best Garden at Castle Bromwich, where the remains of a mid-Victorian *parterre* could be clearly identified close to the surface in an area still cultivated for roses. In this case the beds were largely oval features cut into a dumped layer of gravel, which acted as a hard standing surface to make the pattern of the beds stand out clearly. In altering this pattern, probably in the 20th century, a relatively thin layer of soil was dumped over the whole and rose cultivation carried out on the new surface. Despite regular maintenance, the gardener having claimed to have undertaken 'double-digging' of the new beds, the entire pattern survived a mere 150mm below the modern ground surface (see Fig 2).

One type of garden feature that can tolerate greater machine digging are terrace dumps. These often involved huge earth moving operations in the past, the terraces regularly being over 1.5m higher than the ground surface below. They were frequently created by 'cut and fill' methods meaning that considerable chunks of archaeology below the terrace will have often been removed. The soil cut away from below the terrace was often used to create the terrace itself further down the slope. If the terrace needs to be explored during an evaluation, it is often permissible to remove these dump layers with machine. The excavator needs to be cautious here to ensure that

64

Figure 30: Coombe Abbey, Warwickshire, 1993. Excavations in the East Garden exposed massive brick foundations to the Elizabethan raised planting beds which quartered the garden. One lies in the foreground. (Copyright Iain Soden)

plant beds were not laid out on top of the terrace. After the topsoil has been removed, it would be prudent to trowel back the surface for a few successive spits to see if there are plant beds on the terrace. If none are found, and it seems that the terrace was laid out simply as a grassed over feature, the machine can then be brought back to remove the dump layers carefully. Caution needs to be exercised again as the digging approaches the old ground surface, for this will need to be hand excavated as it is likely to be a very important horizon that may contain not only dating evidence for the period before the terrace was laid out, but also potential evidence for environmental sampling that could inform the excavators about the pre-terrace botanical environment. When working on a garden site, any potential for recovering historic botanical information should be given a high priority.

Depending on the age of the terrace, the cut away area below the terrace areas can build up further levels of archaeology as the surfaces there undergo successive changes in garden plan. This can lead to some odd looking archaeology, with relatively later stratigraphy dropping straight on to undisturbed geology, without any intervening layers in between. At Castle Bromwich, the original formal terraces were once much lower than they are today. The revetment wall in front of the middle terrace was found to be deeply buried, indicating it once had far more of its face exposed. In the 1820s the flights of steps leading down the terraces were removed, and glacis slopes put in to replace them. Below the Middle Terrace the ground levels were built up by around a metre, and a new gravel walk known as the Holly Walk laid down. This latter feature caused much controversy, as the garden management felt the gravel walk ought to belong to the earlier formal garden period. This was not the case and any 'Holly Walk' described earlier must have been a grass walk at a much greater depth. Sealed below the later gravel were sherds of late 18th- or early 19th-century creamware that confirmed the archaeological interpretation, and the unusual depth to which the terrace revetment wall had been buried. As can be seen from Hayden (1993), those involved with the Trust managing the gardens were unable to appreciate the relevance of a 'sealed' layer.

One of the most important facets of multi-phase gardens is their potential to throw up 'sealed' layers. As garden fashion changed, so successive generations often felt obliged to alter the design of a garden. Sometimes this was done by simply digging through the existing garden, and planting anew. For many years archaeologists considered that this was the most likely course of events, and this gave rise to the unwritten, but commonly held opinion, that multi-phase garden sites were unlikely to produce good excavated evidence. This perception of continual redigging of gardens led to a view that archaeological stratigraphy would be so disturbed as to be unworthy of serious attention. Consequently early archaeological explorations tended to concentrate on finding more solid features such as garden structures, which were less susceptible to disturbance. Prior to the Leverhulme Research Project at Castle Bromwich virtually nothing had been published about excavating plant beds. The Castle Bromwich report, produced in 1993, has helped change this view.

Provided with the opportunity of raising the level of the garden, it would seem that historic gardeners would often prefer to 'dump' another layer on top of the older design, and then start again. This was certainly the case in the Best Garden at Castle Bromwich. Here the terraced layout gave scope for at least five successive phases to be dumped one on top of the other, often with limited disturbance to the one below. This situation gave considerable scope for recovering 'sealed' layers, particularly as gravel

Figure 31: Chiswick House Cascade, London. Designed by William Kent for Lord Burlington. The cascade, at the eastern end of a serpentine lake, was of six arches, in two rows of three separated by a carriage drive. The photograph shows the southernmost of the three upper arches with a lead-lined basin at the foot of the arch and the stub of a lead pipe which supplied water from below. Contrary to contemporary engravings, the cascade did not spout water and appears never to have worked satisfactorily (Copyright Northamptonshire Archaeology and English Heritage)

paths and hard standings comprised of compacted layers made contamination from above difficult. Where such compacted areas overlaid previous plant beds their value as a sealing agent was doubled as botanical sampling was an obvious option. Even at Hampton Court, where the Privy Garden was not laid out on a terrace, the well-preserved remains of the garden of 1701–02 had survived both the redesign of the garden in the later centuries, and the considerable potential damage from roots caused by the overgrown yews and other plants that were there prior to the excavation (Dix & Parry 1995, 79). It was even more surprising that traces of beds were found at The Workhouse, Southwell, where there was no evidence at all of subsequent dumping, and the garden had been dug throughout its life from the one level (Currie 1999). A similar situation was encountered by Robert Bell at Painswick, Gloucestershire. Despite a large amount of modern earth-moving, he was still able to trace some of the paths in the kitchen garden (Bell 1993, 35).

A contrast with the terraced Best Garden at Castle Bromwich was provided by the North Garden. Only a single trial trench was cut within it to evaluate its potential during the Leverhulme Project. The North Garden was not built on a terrace as such, it being set on relatively level ground between the hall and the parish church. In some ways the archaeological survival did not have the potential of the remains in the Best Garden. Nevertheless the *parterre* here was set out in a similar manner to the Best Garden, in that the beds were cut into a dumped layer of compacted gravel. Although there was little evidence for subsequent dumping to start a new design, the later gardens being cut through the same level, survival was still of a reasonable standard. This was largely because the dumped surface of the original *parterre* was so compacted that later gardeners found it difficult to dig through thoroughly. As the laying down of hard surfaces, with the beds cut into that surface, was a common technique in the construction of 17th- and early 18th-century *parterres*, there is considerable potential for the survival at Castle Bromwich to be repeated on other sites. From the limited work done elsewhere, it would seem that the survival of garden features, even in unpromising situations like the Southwell Workhouse, can often be greater than expectations.

Briefs for developer-led evaluation only occasionally contains provision for geophysics (see chapter 6), so the excavator is often required to use informed guesswork in laying out trenches. If we imagine that there are no clues to the earlier design from other sources, the worst one could do is lay trenches out so that they are given an even spread across the site. Do not stick rigidly to your proposed layout if the results of the first few trenches show that the evaluation would be best served by changing the position of the later trenches. There is nothing wrong with changing your mind, but make sure that any alterations are carefully thought out and not panic reactions to a project that seems to be going wrong.

In many cases evaluations are carried out to seek specific information about a particular garden feature. Sometimes the approximate location is known, and a linear trench across the approximate location of that feature will often give clues to its position even if it does not find it. For example, if the target feature is a structure, a spread of rubble located at one end of the trench may indicate that the position is nearby, and another trench can be opened up to explore this possibility.

For the most part evaluation is undertaken by linear trenches. The width of these vary depending on the requirements of the planning authority curator. These days most curators ask for the trenches to be between 1.2m and 2m width. Often they ask for them to be 'bucket width', usually meaning the width of a 1.6m standard wide ditching bucket used by 360 degree machines. Such widths are acceptable for many garden projects, but curators should not be so dogmatic on garden sites as they might be on more general sites. Two metres is probably the maximum that one would require on most garden evaluations. Considering that many garden features are of a linear type, there is an argument that trenching, especially on formal garden sites, should be restricted to 1m or less so that the overall spread of the trenching can cover greater areas. There should always be contingencies in the project design to shorten the total length of trenching in order to widen those trenches that show potential for useful information beyond the confines of the designated width.

Many garden sites allow for quite narrow trenches to be dug, especially when trying to find the location of paths. If machines are to be used, it is rare that a ditching bucket can be obtained that will dig a trench narrower than 0.8m, except on very small machines of around one or two tons. Such machines are generally not powerful enough for the majority of evaluations where considerable quantities of earth need to be moved to satisfy the planning brief. It is rare that machines under three ton are used for archaeological evaluation. The nature of the machine depends on the extent of trenching required. In general, the author prefers not to use the largest machines on garden sites, as these can cause considerable damage. The author's policy is to use the smallest machine capable of doing the job, normally a machine in the 3–5 ton range. Whereas 360 degree tracked machines are undoubtedly the most efficient, these can cause much damage on garden lawns etc, and in this case a wheeled JCB-type machine can sometimes be less damaging.

There are going to be times when the client is going to have objections to the use of machinery. Usually if the job is part of the planning process it is likely that the site is going to be damaged by the subsequent development, and the client will not object to machinery being used. On certain sites, the use of machinery will be forbidden or severely limited, and the level of reinstatement required may make their use prohibitive in terms of cost. In such cases the only recourse is to hand-dig the trenches. This can also be a problem if the planning authority requires 300m of trenching and the client is adamant that the site should be fully restored. In such cases, my advice is to inform the planning authority of the problem and let it come to a compromise agreement with the owner that does not involve you becoming entangled in undertaking an impractical brief. It is important that all excavating archaeologists should be aware of the potential for conflict between standard evaluation requirements and those of the garden managers. Although the majority of the author's work in gardens has been done by hand, an increasing number of them in recent years have been done by machinery. There have been no cases where a sensible compromise on the use of machinery has not been arranged.

In cases where path location is required, it is often better not to use a machine at all. At both Leigh Park and The Wakes, both Hampshire, work has been carried out to locate paths that required very narrow trenches. At Leigh Park, the paths were so close to the surface that they could be located by probing with surveyor's arrows. If it is only the alignment of the path that is required, trenches as narrow as a spade width (0.3m) can be acceptable. If a bit more detail on the path's make-up is required, a width of 1m is often sufficient. At Castle Bromwich test trenches to locate plan details were restricted to hand-dug trenches only 0.7m wide. This enabled long trenches to be dug to give an overall section through the site. One such trench was 50m long. The

Figure 32: Castejones Palace, Agreda, Spain. Built by don Diego Gonzalez de Castejon y Vinuesa in the 16th century the palace has survived largely intact though the garden has undergone many changes. Some of the formal outline remained intact, including the arched niche shown. Geophysical survey and excavation revealed the demolished sections of the walled enclosed garden though due to former deep cultivation no planting evidence survived. This was the first garden archaeology known to the author to be carried out in Spain (Copyright Northamptonshire Archaeology and Citeria)

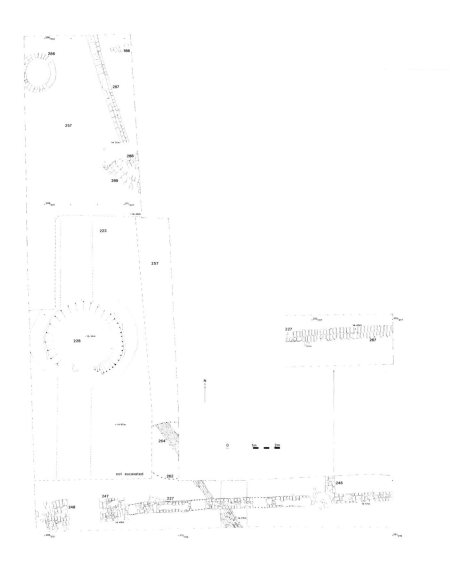

Figure 33: Drawing of the excavation results from the main trench at Upper Lodge showing multi-phase features. In 1709 this area became the site of the Central Basin of Lord Halifax's water garden, but there were negligible remains of this feature. Interpretation: 287/288 edge of pre-1709 lodge?, 264/289 pre-1709 drains, 247/248 gate piers leading into pre-1709 walled garden compartments, 227/246/267 pre-1709 garden walls. In the late 19th century a short-lived concrete fountain was set in front of the new lodge (228). (For full interpretation refer to Currie et al 2003)

71

effort saved on not digging this trench at the standard 1m width was quite considerable, and allowed far greater areas to be trenched within the limited budget. This is about as narrow as a true evaluation trench should be allowed to go, and it is only with regard to finding paths and other linear features that the very narrow trenches described above are useful. If the initial digging is to be carried out by machine 1m should be the minimum width of trenches.

In conclusion, it would seem that linear trenching provides the best initial results in gardens. Area excavation only needs to be resorted to when there is a need to expand test trenches that have indicated places where this would be useful. Total excavation of a garden area should be avoided if possible, as on any archaeological site, as there may be a need to test the results in the future, as was demonstrated at Kirby Hall (Dix *et al* 1995, 296). Excavating machinery should be used with caution, as features like plant beds can have delicate survival close to the surface that can be removed with a single scoop if one is not aware of this relatively common phenomenon. However, with care and experience, machinery can be used successfully even where such features exist, as was shown at the Southwell Workhouse (Currie 1999; see case studies).

(See end of Section for notes)

Chapter 9: Environmental sampling

Environmental sampling has long been a standard technique for any excavation. Soil samples are taken from promising contexts in the hope that macro- and micro-fossils will be present that can give a clue to the characteristics of past environments. All sorts of faunal and botanical remains can be found in archaeological soils that can aid this investigation. The list of artefacts that can be collected is vast, and it keeps growing as new methods are invented. The most common materials collected are animal bone, molluscs, seed, pollen, wood, charcoal and insects, but as sampling becomes more sophisticated so we might include spores, algae, bacteria, phytoliths and parasites. The list is almost endless, and for further details the readers should refer to a standard text (Shackley 1981, Pearsall 1989, Orton 2000, English Heritage 2002).

As well as the remains found within the soil, considerable information about the environment of a garden can be obtained from soil analysis. There is a wide spectrum of tests that can be applied to soils from a simple pH test to determine the acidity or alkalinity of the soil through to particle and complex chemical analysis.

It is soil analysis, seed recovery and pollen analysis that is likely to offer the most information from a garden site, and it is these subjects that will form the majority of this chapter. Before moving on to this, it is worth making some comment on the most popular staple of the environmental archaeologist, the collection of animal bone.

SAMPLING METHODS IN GARDENS

The size of the samples taken tends to vary. For general environmental work that involves wet sieving for bone, seed and general macrofossils the trend has been moving ever upwards. This has not been popular with everyone, although, no doubt environmentalists would be very content. Shortly after the recent guidelines came out from English Heritage, a local authority curator phoned me to solicit my support against the recommendation that 'sample size will normally be of the order of 40–60 litres' (English Heritage 2002, 20). This did seem a rather impractically large sample to take in many circumstances so the advice of a current independent environmentalist was sought, and it seemed that this was acceptable to her. Nevertheless the curator in question seems to have had good reason to want to contest this figure. Apparently he felt that the size was impractical 'as standard' for archaeological evaluations and watching briefs, and that the figure given was only applicable to research work. It might further be questioned whether such figures are more applicable to sampling for bone on more general sites, and might often be excessive in garden contexts where seed is normally the only material where bulk samples are required.

When the Leverhulme Project at Castle Bromwich was underway, we were recommended to take five litres for seed recovery. In retrospect, it is possible that results might have been better if we had taken more. Certainly over the years the author was more inclined to try to increase the chances of a good result by taking ten litres or more. This never seemed to make very much difference to the overall results, although there are bound to be exceptions. The problem with garden sites is that it is very difficult to find a context worth sampling that contains anywhere near 60 litres of soil. In the case of smaller features the English Heritage guidelines recommend taking 100%. The guidelines do state that in specialist conditions the sample size for plant remains can be in the order of 20 litres. In an earlier article the view had been expressed that whereas 50 litres would be need for bulk soils, between five and ten litres might be applicable in certain cases of well-sealed features (de Moulins & Weir 1997, 41).

One of the leading principles behind my own sampling was to avoid contamination. To this end the team would clean the feature until all residual soil from other features was removed. We would then quickly remove the top part of the context and discard it to be absolutely sure we were in the undisturbed feature. Only then would we sample. Often five to ten litres was as much as we could get before we were in danger of impinging on other contexts.

We tended to take the samples from the feature 'in plan' rather than from the section. The English Heritage guidelines seem to imply samples are best taken from sections using monolith tins or Kubiena boxes. We started sampling like this but found it was often impractical in gardens simply because the plant beds we were sampling tended to be discrete features, often sealed beneath other features such as paths. Many plant beds do not lend themselves to sampling in section. Also only large planting holes are likely to be of any great size. By the time you have reduced the soil to ensure contamination is minimal, ten litres would often be a good sized sample. The message that is being made here is the sampler must try to take into account the practicalities of the task in hand.

It is almost impossible to pre-judge which contexts are likely to recover good macrofossil evidence on garden sites. Survival is rarely dependent on natural conditions in gardens because they are frequently poor. It is the alteration of specific plant beds through enhancement that often creates the conditions that allow seed to survive in gardens. Because of this it is almost inevitable that sampling will have to be evaluated first on a garden site: there is no point in hampering the project with guidelines that have been written mainly for non-garden conditions. The evidence on successfully sampled garden sites to date (admittedly, few in number) suggests that sample sizes should be dictated by the project's needs and practicalities in the evaluative stages. If you have fantastic survival, you are unlikely to be able to take a sample that is too big, but don't get bogged down in guidelines. They are there to 'guide', not to coerce you into working in an impractical or clumsy manner.

With certain specialist sampling such as for soils or pollen, much smaller quantities can be taken. Pollen samples seldom need to be more than 50 grms. English Heritage (*ibid*) state that 1–2cm^3 is sufficient for pollen. Take more than this in case mistakes are made on the first analysis, and it needs to be checked; 25–50grms should be enough. For soil analysis 5 grms was sufficient for the Leverhulme analyst to obtain excellent results, although this made the author nervous, and the author would prefer to give 25–50 grms. English Heritage suggest 0.5 litre for soil particle analysis (*op cit*). The general principle is established here that soil and pollen analysis does not require unwieldy sample sizes. Consult your specialist on their requirements.

Figure 34: Castle Bromwich Hall, West Midlands: seeds recovered from the first season of sampling in 1989

Animal bone

In general these remains have not been published in archaeological reports on gardens. Soil, seed and pollen are all mentioned in published specialist reports for Hampton Court, but there is no bone report. Bone is only referred to in the analysis of macroscopic remains in so far as fragments of burnt bone were found in the garden soils that might have been deliberately introduced as fertiliser (Robinson 1995, 115). To date only brief bone reports have appeared in the reports for Kirby Hall, Northamptonshire and Castle Bromwich, West Midlands.

The Kirby excavation found high levels of bone residuality in the garden, and it was suggested that much of it was redeposited medieval material from the destroyed village that had underlain the hall. Hylton (1995, 370) expressed the view that it was unlikely large quantities of waste bone would have been tolerated in the garden whilst it was under cultivation.

A slightly longer report was produced by Locock (1993e) on the bone from Castle Bromwich. This does not mention residuality, and seems to feel that the assemblage was related to the estate, and may have ended up in the garden via the compost bin. Locock also felt that the acidic nature of the soils might have a bearing on the assemblage, and undertook some analytical work on the chemical change in the buried bone (Locock *et al* 1992). This discovered that soil pH might not necessarily be the prime factor in bone decay, and even in supposedly good conditions bone survival is often just a percentage of the original assemblage. This might be reflected in the samples from Castle Bromwich that were wet sieved. An additional 444 small bones were recovered here, with frog and vole being noted in the West Pond backfill. There was no evidence for any loss of species resulting from the acidic nature of the soil (Locock 1993a, 187).

The conclusion to be drawn here is that bone assemblages from garden sites tend to be more fragmented than might be expected on a more general site. This probably results from a conscious effort to keep domestic waste out of garden areas whilst they are under cultivation. The most notable exception could be the use of ground or burnt bone in garden soils as a fertilisers, but to date there has been no conclusive evidence for this in archaeological contexts.

Soil analysis

There are many different approaches to soil analysis. In the past the most common tests used have been spot testing for phosphate, pH testing and particle size analysis.

The latter was once considered a standard requirement for all soil analysis, but it is now recognised to have rather limited applications (Shackley 1981, 17). Although particle size analysis was tested at Castle Bromwich, it was found to provide limited information. For instance it was able to distinguish between water-lain silts in a pond and soils subsequently thrown in during the back-filling of that feature. Unfortunately the archaeologists on site had already determined this from visual inspection of the same soils; the particle size analysis merely confirmed what was already known (Currie & Locock 1991a, 86). Nevertheless there may be occasions where visual inspection of soils will not be sufficient, and on such occasions soil sampling could prove useful. The method was used at Hampton Court and showed certain soils had been imported (Macphail, Crowther & Cruise 1995, 116–18).

Phosphate and pH testing have long been a recognised method of soil testing in archaeology. In theory much has been expected from phosphate testing. This is based on the hypothesis that wherever people settle, their activities will increase the phosphate content of the soils in their vicinity. This is done by lighting fires and producing phosphate by burning wood, by discarding organic materials around habitation areas (waste food, bone, faeces), and deliberately enhancing soils to provide better crop yields (manuring and composting). This type of testing is frequently undertaken in conjunction with pH test, as the pH of the soil (a measure of its acidity/alkalinity) can also be altered by human activity. In reality, phosphate testing has been undertaken with mixed results. This resulted in Shackley (1981, 37) commenting:

> Much lateral variation [in phosphate content] exists and one of the major archaeological needs is to ensure that the total horizontal and vertical range of sediments present on the site is examined. New analytical methods need to be developed and care taken in evaluating the results of phosphate analysis of archaeological contexts by traditional methods since these may be producing values which represent only a certain type of soil phosphorus[8]

It was with this statement in mind that the Leverhulme Project attempted to come up with methods of soil analysis that might help overcome these existing problems, and provide a series of tests that would be specifically useful in gardens. It is believed that this was achieved, although the eventual refinement of the basic methods put forward below can probably be improved upon if specialists in the field could be encouraged to examine them.

The initial soil tests undertaken at Castle Bromwich (Currie & Locock 1991a, 84–87) identified that testing for calcium and magnesium, as well as for pH and phosphate, offered increased scope in garden contexts over phosphate testing alone. It is also possible that other elements essential to plant growth, such as potassium, could be tested for with some hope of success.

The theory behind the tests are explained elsewhere (Currie & Locock 1991a, 87), and need not be repeated at length here. Phosphate would have been added to garden soils as enhancement in a number of forms, the best known being animal manure. Calcium could have been added to acidic soils in the form of lime to increase the range of plants grown, and to improve the soil. Heavy composting would also be expected to increase calcium in the soil over time, as rotted plant material is high in that element. Magnesium was added in the form of ash and charcoal, and from composting. The tests rested on the hypothesis that areas of intensive horticulture would be expected to have soils of higher quantities of these elements than untreated soils in the same locality. Comparative sampling should also be able to locate areas of more intensive enhancement within gardens, and thus distinguish between possible past usage of areas abandoned, or where changes are suspected to have taken place.

The graph in Figure 35 gives some idea of how well these comparisons worked at Castle Bromwich. These figures are based on averages from samples taken within a

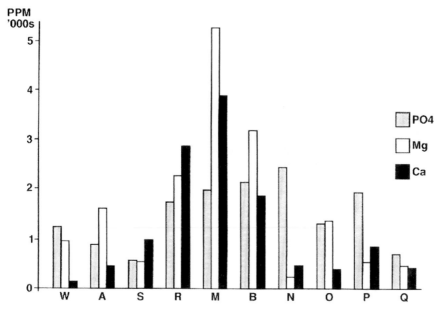

Figure 35: Graph showing resultsof soil tests from various compartments at Castle Bromwich. Key: W – Wilderness, A – Archery Lawn, S – Lower Shrubbery, R – Rose Garden, M – Melon Ground, B – Best Garden, N – North Garden, O – Outer/Slip Garden, P – Parkland, Q – Quarry hollows in park, PPM – parts per million; based on averages from multiple samples taken from each compartment.

given area. It is accepted that such comparison gives a simplistic view of the results, and the conclusions were not drawn from these comparisons alone. Nonetheless, the results demonstrate clear differences between areas that were wilderness and shrubbery, from lawns, and from a variety of different plant beds. The results from the soils in the Melon Ground, where enhancement was probably at its greatest (the beds here were interpreted as hot beds), was significantly higher than the relatively poor soils found in the wilderness/shrubbery areas. The latter probably derived from quarries nearby as these areas sat on built up terraces. Readings obtained from samples taken from the wilderness/shrubbery areas were similar to those taken from known quarry hollows in the park. The relatively high values in some areas of the parkland outside the garden derives from the possibility of the soils being from former arable land. Degenerate ridge-and-furrow can be found outside the garden walls, and is suspected beneath the lower terrace within the garden.

The above soil tests could be particularly useful on abandoned garden sites, as well as those where changes have taken places in the past. It could also help archaeologists to interpret difficult features where no other clues are forthcoming as to their previous use.

TABLE 9.1: comparison of soils from suspected plant beds and path at Oak House.

	pH	Phosphate	Magnesium	Calcium
Suspected path	7.11	702	199	666
Suspected plant bed	6.97	1227	193	2096

At Oak House, West Midlands, what was believed to be a small garden of the first half of the 17th century was buried beneath up to 1m of industrial waste to form a late 19th century municipal bowling green. What were thought to be paths were found. These were made of sand laid into a shallow trench, and cambered for drainage. The soils alongside these paths were thought to a plant beds, possibly grass plats. Because sand alone is an unusual surface on a path that appeared to be for walking (all other garden paths found by excavation were gravel or paved stone) it was thought desirable to test the soil against that of the suspected bed alongside it. The results showed that the bed soil had probably been enhanced, whereas that in the path had not. This helped confirm the original interpretation (Currie & Locock 1991b)

As with all new techniques, the method has not been without its problems. Although the testing of specific contexts does not present any major problems, further research is still required to establish the best methodology for spot testing large areas. This is particular necessary if the technique is to be used on abandoned garden sites. Nevertheless, soil testing for the combination of elements designated above proved to be a significant advance in the archaeological interpretation of gardens. Other researchers' work on non-garden sites, using phosphate testing alone, has often proved inconsistent. The work at Castle Bromwich has shown that multiple-element tests give a much more coherent picture of what has gone on in the past. Tests at other garden sites have subsequently confirmed the method's usefulness. The potential for use on non-garden sites should also be noted (Currie 1995b).

One of the potential criticisms of the soil tests undertaken at Castle Bromwich was whether the differences between soil types would stand up to statistical analysis. In this respect, a student at Bournemouth University, under the supervision of John

Beavis, a specialist in soil analysis, made some statistical tests at Leigh Park, where the tests had seemed to have worked (Currie 1995a).

Amongst the tests made here was an analysis of soils within the cultivated area of the walled garden (sample E/4), soils from beneath a path (sample E/3) and a control sample from outside the garden (sample E/1). The provisional spot testing produced the following results:

Sample no	pH	inorganic Phosphate	calcium	magnesium
E/1	6.60	141.7	293	504.3
E/3	7.09	1428.7	6419	707.3
E/4	7.11	1850.5	7829	769.5

Further statistical tests were then carried out by Bournemouth University that concluded that the differences between the above contexts were statistically valid, indicating that the testing method recommended here does have a scientific basis (Yulle-Baddeley 1994).

Since the above tests were carried out soil analysis using different tests (pH, phosphate & carbonate) were carried out at Hampton Court, which showed differentiation between different garden soils and non-garden soils (Macphail, Crowther & Cruise 1995, 116–18).

The overall conclusion is that soil testing on gardens is worthwhile in helping to determine the type of activity undertaken in different areas. Collection for these tests is simplicity itself. The Castle Bromwich project used small screw-top plastic tubes provided by the project biochemist, Stephen Gray. These are used to take samples for medical research, but any sealable container could be used. Very little soil is required to complete a test. We were collecting about 20 grms, but this may be too small a quantity if the tests need to be repeated. A sample of around 50 grms should be sufficient, although the reader should take advice from their environmental specialist on this, as the needs of individual specialists may vary.

All the author's soil tests were undertaken by Stephen Gray, who used Atomic Absorption Spectrophotometry to test the soil's chemistry. Readers interested in the methodology are referred to Hughes *et al* (1976) or the British Museum's Scientific Research pages at
http://www.thebritishmuseum.ac.uk/science/techniques/sr-tech-aas.html.

Botanical Sampling

Macrofossils (seed)

Many garden soils are of an acidic nature in their natural state, and they would not normally be expected to preserve seed (Shackley 1981, 163–5; Murphy and Scaife 1991, 85). The soil tests described above were instrumental in showing that garden soils were seldom left in their natural state, and it was common to enhance them to suit the requirements of the plants that the gardeners wanted to grow. This led to some unexpectedly encouraging results from sampling at Castle Bromwich. Subsequent work elsewhere seemed to support the idea that sampling garden soils for seed

Figure 36: Castle Bromwich Hall, West Midlands: column sampling for soil analysis in the early days of the Leverhulme research.

can be worthwhile. Nevertheless, it has to be said that sampling as a matter of course is likely to give only random successes. In North America, where they have had success in garden archaeology over a longer period than in the UK, the general view is that it 'is the stratigraphic sequence and archaeological context that determines the usefulness of botanical data' (Yentsch & Kratzer 1997, 48). This author has found that to be consistently successful archaeologists need to target their sampling on beds that have been enhanced. It should be noted that the 'engineering' of soils in plant beds is often to decrease acidity, so that most enhanced soils are likely to be less acidic than the parent soil. It is this enhancement that creates micro-environments within plant beds that are likely to preserve seed.

The background to this sampling is given in Currie and Locock (1991a, 87–89). The total seed count from 36 five-litre soil samples at Castle Bromwich (of which 26 produced plant remains; a 72% success rate) was 1183 individual seeds from dated historic contexts. Of these 475 were identified to individual species, 594 to *genus* (e.g. *Triticum* sp. rather than the specific *Triticum aestivum*), 16 to family only, and 98 were unidentified. A total of 22 different species were identified.

It should be noted that many of the species identified were either cereals, common weeds or native wild flowers. Although some of the latter were known to have been cultivated in gardens, they were more likely to have been growing wild. This should not be unexpected as garden plants, by their very nature, are not often allowed to go to seed. On initial inspection, these results may not seem to have been particularly useful, but, in fact, relevant information was obtained. More importantly, it was shown that the method could produce useful results far more consistently than

80

previously expected. It had previously been thought that acid garden soil would destroy seed remains, and sampling would not be worthwhile. In fact Murphy and Scaife (1991, 85) had expressed the pessimistic view that ' ... garden soils are the very last place one would normally expect to find identifiable macrofossils [seeds]'.

At Castle Bromwich, a pit of medieval date was especially interesting in identifying a wide range of food crops that must have been grown in the vicinity. Amongst those recognised were *Triticum aestivum* (wheat), *Secale* sp. (rye), *Pisum* sp. (pea), and *Pyrus/Malus* sp. (pear or apple), as well as a large number of cereal and legume seeds that were not further identified. This evidence was instrumental in identifying Castle Bromwich as a demesne centre in the Middle Ages. Previous research had suggested that the manor house lay elsewhere, and that the first house on the site had been built around 1600. Documentary research partly confirmed the idea of an earlier use of the site by finding a survey of 1575 that identified the hall site as being covered by buildings totalling 23 bays, with two acres of gardens (Locock 1993d, 165–6).

The beds of the earliest gardens contained quantities of cereal seed, as well as *Vicia fabia* (field bean), demonstrating crops grown locally. Other plant remains were found that may have been collected as food crops included *Hordeum vulgare* (hulled barley), *Sambucus nigra* (elderberry), and *Fagus sylvatica* (beech nut). Although elderberry is a common weed that was found throughout the garden, the presence of 43 seeds in a single sample from a sealed pit was considered to be too much to be caused by weeds, and it is possible that this represented the deliberate collection of the fruits.

Cereal remains were recovered from a variety of beds in the garden. These were probably introduced either with bedding straw from the stables (uncharred seeds), indicating manuring as part of the garden management process, or as ashy residues put on plant beds as part of the soil enhancement process (charred seeds). There were tentative suggestions that this was less intensive in the phase II *parterre* garden (*c.* 1700), possibly indicating that this garden may have been less plant-orientated than those before and after.[9] The *parterre* in the Best Garden appears, from other evidence, to have comprised largely a design made up of grass plats and gravel surfaces. Weed seeds after this phase tentatively suggested a period of partial abandonment, a conclusion confirmed by other archaeological and documentary evidence for the years *c* 1747–1818 (Currie and Locock 1993a, 134).

Work on subsequent garden sites has demonstrated that seed can be recovered from a wide variety of sites on different soils across the country. A common factor in this recovery is the presence of cereal seed brought into the garden with manure and composting, and spread on plant beds as soil enhancement. As at Castle Bromwich, weed seed dominated some assemblages, but this should not be seen as surprising as they tend to dominate samples taken from non-garden sites, and the work of sampling for seed invariably requires the sampler to sift through residual material.

The small assemblage from Hanbury Hall did not exhibit the dominance of weeds found on other sites. Here cereal seeds, introduced during soil enhancement, dominated (67.5%), but there was a significant proportion of fruit seeds (20%), including strawberry (*Fragaria ananassa*), raspberry/blackberry (*Rubus fruticosus*) and apple/pear (*Pyrus/Malus* sp.). Weeds provided only 11.3% of this assemblage (de Rouffignac & Currie 1996).

Excavations at the early 19th-century informal landscape at Leigh Park enabled samples to be taken from a series of contexts associated with plant beds from the various thematic gardens scattered across the 800-acre plus landscaped garden. Weed seed dominated this assemblage, suggesting possible contamination in historic times. The numbers of charred seed was quite high here, and cereal seeds were relatively scarce, a situation that contrasted with other sites. Some seeds from ornamental trees no longer present on site were suggested by the presence of hornbeam and walnut. Other than this only fruit seeds of raspberry and strawberry from the Farmhouse and Dutch gardens respectively indicated possible plants grown deliberately (de Rouffignac 1995).

Sampling for seed was undertaken at Hampton Court, the only other purely garden site to have published details of findings. Here the majority of the seed recovered came from holly and yew, both plants used extensively in the historic garden. Only one fruit fragment of box was recovered, and weed seeds were rare (Robinson 1995, 115–16).

Contamination from modern sources is the major problem in interpreting the evidence from garden sites. Even in sealed contexts there is always a possibility of contamination unnoticed by the excavator. The general opinion of the author's own advisors on sampling was that although the evidence needs to be treated with caution, it is certain that potential for seed recovery in garden sites has been demonstrated. The fact that garden soils are frequently enhanced, altering their original nature indicates that assumptions cannot be made that they will not be conducive to survival because many garden soils are 'acidic'. At Castle Bromwich the average pH of the control soils was about 4, yet in the Melon Grounds, where soils where likely to be most enhanced, the pH of the predominantly sand soil was boosted to 8.2.

Environmental sampling has been shown to be a viable method in historic gardens. It is tempting to say 'in the right circumstances' but this might imply that the right type of context can be predicted. The author's experience has suggested that such is the variability of the micro-environments present in separate planting areas in any given garden that it is better not to pre-judge anything until you have evidence to the contrary.

Although the information obtained from the seeds to date has been of more theoretical interest to archaeologists than to garden historians and those involved in drawing up restoration plans, the proof that seeds can be recovered is highly signif-icant. The failure to recover seed from cultivated or exotic plants in large quantities does not detract from the potential of the method, as chance can be a factor deter-mining the type of seed recovered. With persistence, the method has a good probability of succeeding. What is now needed is further research that might identify the type of features that produce consistently, and those that will recover information of a specific kind.

Pollen sampling

Pollen sampling and analysis was another area of research that had received a bad press in gardens prior to the Leverhulme Project at Castle Bromwich. As with sampling for seed, this method had previously been considered to be largely unsuited to garden archaeology because of the special conditions believed to be necessary to preserve pollen (Murphy and Scaife 1991, 90–91). At Aberdour Castle, sampling had proved largely disappointing (Hynd & Ewart 1983, 105), but this contrasts with the results from the Roman garden at Fishbourne, West Sussex. Here, pollen sampling proved to be useful in determining aspects of the garden's environment (Greig 1971). The results at Castle Bromwich also seemed to indicate potential (Currie & Locock 1991a, 89–90; Currie & Locock 1993a). Once again, it seems that garden soils create their own micro-environments that make pre-judgement on survival unwise. The methodology used for sampling is described in Currie and Locock (1991a, 89–90).

The difference between sampling for pollen and for seed is that pollen tends to survive better in acid soils, whereas seed survives better in more alkaline contexts. It might therefore be expected that pollen might survive in contexts not producing seed. Curiously, at Castle Bromwich, some samples contained both seed and pollen, although it is unlikely to obtain optimum recovery of either from such a sample.

As with seed recovery, contamination is a serious problem, and every effort should be made to avoid this. The major problems of pollen sampling are discussed by Faegri and Iverson (1975) and Shackley (1981, 71–92). Readers with a specific interest in this area are referred to the three different procedures for sampling listed by Pearsall (1989, 261–64).

At Castle Bromwich 45 samples were submitted, and 21 contained pollen (46.7%); of these only eight reached the standard count of 500 TLP thought necessary for realistic results. Nevertheless sufficient pollen was obtained to allow worthwhile conclusions to be drawn. Unlike seeds, identification to species level was rare, family or *genus* being the normal limit of accuracy.

The results were of some interest with regard to earlier land uses, and were able to identify probable abandonment of arable cultivation and reversion to pasture at an undefined pre-garden phase. Within the garden itself, a period of abandonment, or semi-managed grassland was evidenced from quantities of *Compositae Liguliflorae* (probably dandelion) within a high proportion of samples. This suggests that large areas of the garden were laid down to managed grassland. This is confirmed by the presence of grass plats in the Best Garden *parterre* from c 1700–1818, and the large lawned area known as the Archery Lawn (c. 180m by 20m). There would appear to have been a period, probably c 1747–1818, when the gardens were neglected; again other archaeological and documentary evidence has confirmed this.

The pollen evidence also reinforced the evidence of the seeds for manuring of *plant* beds. Cereal pollen was present in some samples indicating that it was being brought into the garden attached to bedding straw mixed with animal dung used as plant manure. This is further suggested by the high presence of *Pteridium* (bracken) spores, also believed to have been used as animal bedding, and thus introduced in the same manner.

Certain pollen types could almost certainly be attributed as coming from garden plants. Samples from contexts adjacent to the present Holly Walk showed that *Ilex* (holly) and *Juglans* (walnut) were present in earlier gardens. The most interesting find was 19.2% *Papilionaceae* pollen from a sealed eighteenth-century plant bed in the Melon Ground. This pollen type was not found in significant quantities anywhere else in the garden, and this confirms the earlier supposition that this represents either a legume deliberately cultivated in that bed, or one cultivated elsewhere, and the after-crop residue being introduced as compost. (Currie & Locock 1991a, 90).

To examine the possibility of pollen washing through the sandy soils, and being redeposited elsewhere, control samples were taken at vertical intervals from soils in the park outside the garden. These showed that it was possible to differentiate the pollen profiles recovered at different levels, thus indicating that relocation of pollen was negligible.

Testing at other garden sites by the author was restricted to Oak House, Sandwell, West Midlands. Despite limited sampling, the pollen revealed evidence for manuring, and indicated that *Ligustrum vulgare* (privet) may have been grown in the garden there (Currie & Locock 1991b). However, sampling undertaken in the Privy Garden at Hampton Court seemed to confirm that there is potential in the method, with some pollen being recovered from plants that were probably part of the ornamental plantings in the general vicinity. There was little evidence of pollen from the planted shrubs (yew, box) within the garden itself, but this was largely as expected as many ornamental shrubs tend to have poor pollen production, with dispersion being carried out mainly by insects (Scaife 1995, 116).

Pollen sampling can be shown to be a worthwhile exercise in gardens. Although it is generally considered that pollen analysis is more problematic than macrofossil (seed) work because of its increased wind-spread capabilities (Murphy & Scaife 1991, 85), it can produce meaningful results in gardens. As with seed work, this contradicts previous expectations, and it must be concluded that to pre-judge the issue of survival is unwise. Although the results of work undertaken by the author on pollen has not been tried on as many sites as the sampling for seed, it was relatively successful on both sites at which it was tried.

It should be noted that the percentage of successfully sampled contexts was lower than that for seed (46% against 72%). However, this is slightly misleading, as a certain quantity of pollen needs to be present before analysis can be meaningful, whereas only one seed needs to be recovered from an environmental sample for it to be considered a 'success'. One also has to take into consideration the relative costs. At the time of the Castle Bromwich project (1989–92) a successful pollen sample cost about £100 to analyse, whereas the environmental work was being done for as little as £15–20 per sample. It seems the discrepancy in costs has narrowed considerably since this time. Nevertheless the relative extra costs in pollen sampling require that more careful thought needs to be given to this method, particularly as the overall results are often less well defined with regard to species identification. Despite this caveat, pollen sampling should be included in the garden archaeologist's wish-list wherever possible.

Phytoliths

Phytoliths or plant opals are microscopic silica structures which occur in the cells of certain plants, especially grasses. They are formed via the deposition of dissolved silica within or between plants cells, and they can survive when other plant tissues break down (English Heritage 2002, 15). They have only recently been recognised as having potential on archaeological sites. Until fairly recently their usefulness in general archaeology was still being debated (Adkins & Adkins 1982, 219), but there have been more recent advances, and American researchers have reported success in agricultural and garden soils (Pearsall 1989, 343). At Morven, Princeton, New Jersey the dominance of festucoid grasses in the phytolith assemblage was interpreted as being from a lawned area (Yentsch & Kratzer 1997, 49). Nevertheless, the method still has problems associated with it, and most archaeologists would be advised to seek the advice of a specialist before embarking on a sampling programme.

(See end of Section for notes)

Chapter 10: Finds recovery & analysis

There is no reason why the treatment of finds on a garden site should differ from any other archaeological site. The reason for including this chapter is not to expound a methodology for finds recovery, as this should be treated as seriously as on any other site. There may be a need to retain much later finds (eg pottery) than on other types of site because garden excavations are often interested in dating features of a later date than many other sites. A number of garden excavations have been specifically interested in dating 19th- and early 20th-century plant beds. It is rare that more general excavations require attention to such late features, and on many general sites material and features dating to after *c* 1800 are often removed by machine and the finds discarded after a cursory examination. On garden sites it is often necessary to be able to determine the complete evolution of the garden design, and to this end all stratified finds may need to be recorded in the first instance. There are sometimes exceptions, but there needs to be a good justification for them.

In some respects gardens are seldom different from other sites close to larger residences. If one was excavating in the area immediately adjoining a medieval manor house, features such as rubbish pits might be expected. These can occur in garden areas, but, as a rule, they tend to date from before the area was laid out as a garden. It is generally rare (although not unexpected) that rubbish pits are cut into garden soils once the decision has been made to use the space as part of a garden. Pits might be excavated after the garden is abandoned or during periods of neglect, but it is notable that rubbish pits are rare in garden phases. Thus the only rubbish pit found in the Best Garden at Castle Bromwich dated from the medieval period, a period when there was no direct evidence for the area within which the pit was cut being part of a garden in the generally accepted sense.

How, therefore, do the bulk of finds come to end up in a garden? The process is very similar to how pottery sherds and other finds come to be found in arable fields at great distances from the nearest residence. Most garden finds tend to be deposited in the garden during the manuring or composting processes used to enrich the soil. Botanical analysis of garden soils frequently recover cereal seed, and this has been interpreted as finding its way into the garden from the stable. Inadvertently mixed with the straw used in animal bedding, the dung and soiled bedding was subsequently deposited on a midden before being brought out into the garden. In between broken pottery and other small materials may have found their way into the midden and were consequently added to the garden soils. However, it should be stressed that this rubbish was often present on a small scale, as gardeners wanted their gardens to be neat, and only unobtrusive rubbish would be tolerated. The result is that pottery sherds in garden soils tend to be small. It is rare to get the large chunks of pottery that are often found in rubbish pits and other non-garden contexts.

The exception to this rule is the flowerpot. These are amongst the most common pottery finds in a garden, for obvious reasons. It did not seem to be such a problem to gardeners to throw quite large chunks of broken flowerpot into a bush where it could later be incorporated into the garden soil. Many gardens actually contain flowerpot 'middens', where large quantities of broken vessels were deposited.

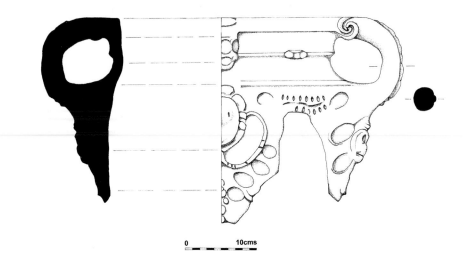

0 _____ 10cms

Figure 37: An elaborate horticultural urn in beige earthenware from Gosport (Hants).
This example is similar to a published example from Ham House, Surrey, dated to the
17th century (Currie 1995d). Both were painted white to imitate stone. The Gosport
example shows such wares were used in town gardens as well as at high status sites.

To the average archaeologist the study of flowerpots is often thought of as a subject
of amusement, and the discarding of such sherds without even cursory study is
commonplace on many sites. With regard to large quantities of mass-produced and
relatively modern wares, this might be acceptable, but the excavator needs to be certain
that the materials really are as recent as they seem. One of the first things an excavator
learns on a garden site is that what appear to be 'modern' flowerpot sherds can often be
crucial dating evidence. All too often these 'modern' sherds are much older than they
seem to be on first impression because flowerpot fabrics can be deceptively similar from
the early 17th century onwards, possibly even earlier. Often the difference between
dating a piece of unglazed red earthenware to the 17th rather than the 20th century lies
in subtle differences in form or fabric. In the London Museum stores, for example, are
examples of London Redware flowerpots dating from the late 16th or early 17th century
that look little different to crude 20th-century pots (pers obs).

This author has made a provisional study of flowerpot types (Currie 1993), and
worked out a rough chronology for these artefacts. Since then further studies have
helped to elaborate on our understanding of the subject. At Ham House, Surrey,
flowerpots from the later 17th century included an outstanding zoomorphic vessel
alongside other vessels barely different from 20th-century forms (Currie 1995d). More
recently Nigel Melton and the late Keith Scott (Melton & Scott 1999) have published a
post-medieval kiln site at Polesworth, north Warwickshire, that contained a considerable number of horticultural wares. Anyone interested in garden excavation should
be aware of this site. This work, together with the discussion in Currie (1993), has

helped to establish a wide range, not only of conventional flowerpots, but numerous other specialist vessels used in horticulture such as earthenware saucers, seed trays, and kale pots, the latter often mistaken for chimney pots.

Early flowerpots had a tendency to have hooked rims to facilitate lifting, particularly in the large sizes. These wares often had drainage holes at the side. Although the central drainage hole that is ubiquitous in modern wares was not unknown in the 17th century, multiple side drainage holes (often between 3 and 4 near the base) were the more common norm. This began to change around the middle of the 18th century, when modern forms begin to appear. Nevertheless, in the West Midlands it was still possible to distinguish late 18th- and 19th- century wares from 20th-century mass-produced pots by a characteristic maroon slip that was painted over the exterior of the pot. Rims on these vessels tended to be folded rather than straight. Although all the characteristics of flowerpots before about 1830 can be found in more modern varieties, earlier flowerpots do have characteristics that aid dating. Considering that domestic pottery generally only finds its way into gardens in small, often undiagnostic, pieces, the information obtained from the study of flowerpot sherds is vital to the interpretation of a garden.

The recent discovery of another elaborate horticultural urn in a pit in a backland area of Gosport (Hants) has helped to advance the study of horticultural wares considerably (Ponsford 2004, in press). This vessel had many similarities with the zoomorphic urn found at Ham House. Unfortunately the damage sustained to the vessel made it uncertain if the relief faces that decorated it were human or monkeys. Nevertheless the decoration included relief and thumb-pressed foliage akin to the Ham vessel, as was evidence for over-painting the vessel white to make it appear as if it were stone. Furthermore, the vessel appeared to be in a similar white clay fabric as that found at Ham, and might suggest that there was a kiln that specialised in the production of such wares.

This discovery is of particular interest as there was a time when garden historians considered that large highly-decorated horticultural urns frequently seen in post-medieval illustrations were only produced in lead and stone. Ordinary terracotta urns, it was considered, would not have been practical as they were prone to be shattered by frost.[10] The Ham and Gosport urns show that they were specialised earthenware vessels made of a similar fabric that produced ordinary everyday wares throughout the 16th and 17th centuries. These vessels further hint that horticultural vessels may have become more simplified over the post-medieval period. Moorhouse (1991, 101–06) has shown that some highly elaborate plant holders were made in the late medieval period, again with relief designs. Similar vessels to these medieval wares were found in excavation at Basing House, where they are now thought to date to after the Civil War phase (post-1650). It is perhaps no coincidence that the Ham vessel was dated to around the same period. Although the Gosport vessel was found in a later pit, its similar fabric suggests it was of the same approximate date as that from Ham. It is possible that such elaborate ceramic vessels may once day prove relatively commonplace. The Gosport vessel was found in the garden in a small Hampshire town, and would therefore have ornamented a rather modest garden. If such gardens were using such elaborate vessels, it might be expected that they would be found readily in the larger gardens of the rich.

Excavators also need to be aware of the wide variety of other ceramic vessels used in gardening. Despite their low tolerance to outdoor conditions, tin-glazed vessels were frequently used in horticulture in the 17th and 18th centuries. An inventory from the Pickleherring potteries dated 1699 records numerous pots made in tin-glazed earthenware for gardens. These are described as 'White and Painted Perfect Ware' and include 'small & midle [sic] Garden potts... butter Garden potts ... sawceers Garden potts... half sawcer flower basons...'(Britton 1990, 110). Although it is very difficult to distinguish between tin-glazed sherds used as garden wares and those used for domestic purposes, this quote should warn the excavator to look out for any large percentages of such fabrics in garden assemblages.

A recent study by Ferguson (1999) has examined the elaborate vessels used in 'indoor' gardening in the 18th century. These were used both for indoor cultivation, as well as for cut flowers. Tin-glazed tiles frequently depicted elaborate urns containing flowers. Those published from Ham House, Surrey (Currie 1995d, fig. 1 nos 5–6) are thought to represent the same tin-glazed wares as the tiles. Contemporary illustrations appear to show tin-glazed vases and urns set on balustrades etc in gardens. Ferguson's work has taken this a stage further and has shown that plant containers were produced that included salt-glazed wares, French porcelain, Coalport porcelain, and English Wedgwood (passim). The article illustrates a pair of white terracotta stoneware garden pots with matching saucers with 'engine-turned flutes and applied festoons' dated 1785–95 from Wedgwood's Etruria pottery. All Ferguson's examples came from museum collections, but there is no reason why such vessels cannot turn up in excavation. Although this research deals largely with pots used for indoor plants, it is possible some of these vessels were used in an outdoor context, particularly on balustrades and terraces close to the house. It is well known that many parterres were decorated with potted plants that were taken into greenhouses etc at night. Under excavation conditions unless a sherd of one of these highly elaborate vessels was recovered containing a drainage hole, it is likely that they would be misidentified as ordinary domestic wares.

Another type of ceramic vessel that can arise in gardens are terracotta ornaments to garden buildings. Terracotta is frequently used on domestic buildings. It is not unknown in a garden context, but has rarely been recovered during excavation to date. One exception are the terracotta shields that William Shenstone used to decorate the Priory Cottage (Ponsford 2000, 306), one of the focal points of his design at The Leasowes in the West Midlands (see chapter 12), found during the excavation of the cottage ruins. All were an off white colour that would have imitated stone from a distance.

Other find types that are peculiar to gardens are plant labels. Modern nurseries use plastic, but in historic times the most common materials were metal. Copper and lead were frequently used and these survive more readily than iron, which often disintegrate so much that the information on them is illegible. Finds of these sorts, with clear markings on them, can often tell us much about the gardening activities and even the plants cultivated. Triangular lead markers were recovered from the garden at Castle Bromwich. These were inscribed with numbers, the latter probably relating to a now lost gardener's notebook (Locock 1993b, 182–3).

Large quantities of window glass are frequently found in garden soils. This is often the result of glass used in greenhouses, or even from individual panes that were positioned around particular types of plant and subsequently broken. Cloches, a purpose-made glass vessel used to contain individual plants, can also be expected from garden soils. These were found at Aberdour Castle (Hynd & Ewart 1983, 104), and were suspected from Castle Bromwich (Locock 1993c, 180–81).

Figure 38: Carl Linnaeus' binominal botanical classification, Uppsala, Sweden. His scientific system is that which remains in use worldwide today. Plant labels in various forms and materials have been recovered from a number of archaeological excavations (for example see Currie & Locock 1991a, 92, Fig 5). (Copyright Iain Soden)

Other artefacts include lost and broken garden tools. To date few of these have been positively identified from garden excavations in the UK, but a good assemblage was recovered from work by the Colonial Williamsburg Project in the USA. A fine collection of different kinds of hoe, rakes and spades were recovered here (Hume 1989, 72–83). A useful illustration of early 18th-century garden tools can be found in F Gentil's *Le Jardinier Solitaire* (1706), reproduced in Currie (1993; fig 1). The Shire book by Kay Sanecki, *Old Garden Tools* (1987) is a useful handbook to aid identification of recovered items of this sort.

Rescue's *First aid for finds* (Watkinson 1987), remains the main source of guidance for the treatment of different types of find, and it is to this work that the reader is referred for further information.

Although it has been stated above that it is generally necessary to collect all stratified finds from a garden site, there are cases for sampling which can be outlined here. Clearly all building material lends itself to selective sampling. There may be cases for collecting all building materials, but if this is suspected, it should be clearly stated in the project design. There is very seldom reason to collect masses of 19th-century and early modern brick, tile and slate from any site, and gardens are no exception. Nonetheless the excavator should be careful how sampling is applied. If other finds are not forthcoming, brick or tile are often the only stratified finds to be recovered from some contexts. In such instances all this material should be collected and examined. We are not talking about masses of brick from a large dump context of late date, but discrete features that require dating. In these cases a date can sometimes be obtained by examining the brick and tile fabrics. These can sometimes be tied in with dated buildings nearby to give a rough idea of the date of a context. At Oak House, West Midlands, it was the mortar bonding the sandstone foundations of a garden building that dated this feature. A sample of the mortar was collected and analysed. It was then found to correspond with the mortar of standing buildings dating from c 1700 (Currie & Locock 1991b). Similar results can be obtained from fabric analysis of brick and tile.

Another type of find that can prove problematic on garden sites is window glass. Some garden sites contain masses of this material, especially where there have been large areas of demolished greenhouses. There is often a limited amount of information that can be obtained from dumped greenhouse glass. At Bantock Park, West Midlands, a 19th-century pond was infilled with the window glass from a large number of greenhouses (Ponsford 2000, 306). The quantity of this material deposited was immense, and all of it was relatively modern. There was good cartographic evidence for the date of the infill of the pond, further confirmed by the dumped glass, so there was little point in collecting anything but the most minimal sample. In this case, there was no need to count and weigh the amount discarded. The quantity was so large that it made excavation very dangerous, and where health and safety is concerned being pedantic about late window glass has to take second place. It is only when you have excavated a large number of garden sites that it can be appreciated how much of a problem greenhouse glass can sometimes be.

Likewise, there are occasions when a large number of relatively recent flowerpots can be encountered. Again selective sampling will be sufficient here, provided the excavator is alert to the possibility of older fabrics being hidden amongst the latter material.

Sampling should always be tempered with common sense and practicability. Nevertheless it is worth bearing in mind that lack of storage space has resulted in many museums having a discard policy that might be too generalised for garden sites. For instance, there tends to pervade the unwritten policy that commonplace late post-medieval pottery is largely unwelcome in museum stores. This author is in full agreement with this on more general sites but there are occasions when this type of pottery is the principal dating evidence for a garden. When you consider this to be the case, the museum should be told clearly why you would prefer finds to be kept that might otherwise be discarded. It might even be necessary to write that retention is important to the dating of the site into the archive where it can be clearly identified by some future administrator wishing to create space. At the same time, it is necessary to be practical, and retaining late finds for their own sake is not to be encouraged, particularly as most museums now impose a charge by the box for archives. Try to ensure that your sampling and finds retention policy is realistic.

SECTION NOTES

1   The letter is quoted in chapter 13.

2   Their addresses are (respectively): www.hmc.gov.uk/nra/nra2.htm, www.a2a.org.uk, www.archivesnetworkwales.info, www.scan.org.uk

3   An example is given in Chapter 17 relating to Dartington Hall.

4   Trees considerably inhibit a GPS signal.

5   A piece of rectangular wooden board of suitable size should be covered firstly by graph paper. This should be secured by masking tape and a piece of matt waterproof draughting film placed over it. This serves as a suitable 'portable' drawing board. I have five of varying sizes depending on the job in hand. I find the largest size I can handle in reasonable comfort to be 80cms by 60cms.

6   Although there is much to be said for measuring trees by EDM.

7   Further details of Locock's work on the brick-makers in the Forest of Arden can be found in Locock (1990b, 1992).

8   Some time after the Leverhulme work had been completed de Moulins & Weir (1997, 41) confirmed that phosphate sampling on its own was problematic, stating that leaching could occur in soils with a pH of between 5 and 8, but soils either side of this range tended to be more stable. Although unaware of these parameters during the Leverhulme tests, the results largely bore out this idea. The Leverhulme project also attempted to determine the rate of phosphate leaching and its affect on garden soils (Currie & Locock 1991, 85), but this was largely a failure.

9   This ties in with the view that formal gardens became more spartan with regard to plants and more architecturally-orientated in their early 18th-century phase. That is the designs were picked out in coloured earths, and ornamented more with statues and plants in pots than with intensely-planted beds.

10   Garden historians do recognise that urns were occasionally made in a specialised terracotta from the mid 18th-century. 'Coade stone' garden ornaments were made from 1769 in a specialised vitrified ceramic that was frost-resistant. From 1843 the Pulhams made garden ornaments in specialised terracotta that was weather-resistant (Symes 1996, 9–11), but these were specialised wares that fall outside the normal definition of pottery.

COLOUR PLATES

1. *Kenilworth Castle, Warwickshire: medieval designed landscape, looking from the site of the medieval Banqueting House across the site of the Great Mere to the castle shows the large extent of some medieval water-based designs.*

2. *Hanbury Hall, Worcestershire: a reconstructed early 18th-century parterre following excavation. The excavation proved the exact alignment of the garden buildings in the background after a contemporary print and plan by the same draughtsmen were at variance.*

3. *Polesden Lacey, Surrey: Margaret Greville was one of the best known of early 20th-century country house hostesses. Here is her Rose Garden superimposed over the skeleton of an earlier walled garden. The tall garden building in the background disguises a water-tank used to water the roses on this hill-top site.*

4. *Dartington Hall, Devon: linear test trenching on the late 17th-century Best Garden terrace, looking out over the 19th-century formal revivalist terraces. In left-hand edge of shot is the start of the ruined arcade shown in Fig. 57.*

5. *Wardour Castle, Tisbury: the grotto in the grounds of the Old Castle. Made by the Payne brothers, the finest grotto builders of the 18th century, this landscape was worked on by Richard Woods and Capability Brown, and includes the ruins of the original medieval castle as part of the later informal landscape of the New Castle.*

6. *Hampton Court Palace, 1994. View north to the Wren palace. The southern half of the garden shows the emptied platte bandes with the northern half, already excavated and levelled with new soil. A central circular fountain remains from the original design and brick footings to flights of steps can be seen in the terraces. Fragments at lower left remain from Henry VIII's water gallery. Extensive documentary evidence comprising plans, building accounts and planting lists, combined with very high survival of the archaeological record makes this restoration one of the most accurate ever carried out. Survival of the archaeology was a happy accident as almost immediately after completion in 1702 the garden was ignored by successive monarchs and the palace ceased largely to be used. Allowed to grow out, the formal planting became a shrubbery, little disturbed. (Copyright Northamptonshire Archaeology and Historic Royal Palaces Agency)*

7. *The garden of Carl Linnaeus (1707–78), Uppsala, Sweden. Restoration has been faithful to his original scientific layout. (Copyright Iain Soden)*

8. *Carl Linnaeus' planting beds. Uppsala, Sweden. (Copyright Iain Soden)*

Plate 1.

Plate 2.

Plate 3.

Plate 4.

Plate 5.

Plate 6.

Plate 7.

Plate 8.

SECTION 3: CASE AND REGIONAL STUDIES

Chapter 11: The formal garden

Garden archaeologists tend to find themselves undertaking work on two broad types of site – that comprising the formal, geometric layout, and that involving the informal, less structured design. There is little question that the formal design is the easier to work on, largely because the more rigid layout allows the archaeologist to predict where features might be. Even when areas of the garden have been heavily disturbed, if part has survived reasonably well, it is often possible to transfer the design from one quadrant into the others and make a reasonable guess of the overall form of the garden.

I) CASTLE BROMWICH HALL

John Kenyon, the editor of *Post-Medieval Archaeology* from 1989 to 1998, considered that Castle Bromwich Hall, West Midlands, was the first garden site to be fully published in the UK (Kenyon 1993, editorial). As this was a formal garden, it stands out as the obvious example to include here as the case study. Furthermore, Castle Bromwich is probably the only major garden site in the UK to be excavated in recent years without the aid of machinery. This site was unique in that it obtained three years of generous funding from the Leverhulme Trust that enabled the 78 trenches excavated between 1989 and 1992 to be dug by hand. The Leverhulme grant required the excavations to test a variety of archaeological methods, and their application for use in historic gardens. A wide range of methods tested most of the modern techniques used in archaeology. Tests included not only excavation techniques, but the application of environmental sampling methods, (testing for bone, seed and pollen survival), soil analysis, geoprospection methods, dating techniques, and building analysis techniques. The opportunity was taken to pioneer many techniques not previously used in the UK, and to formulate and test the project's own methodologies. A provisional report on the results of this work was published in Currie and Locock (1991).

The excavation results were fully published in four stages. First came the report on the excavation of the unusually complete West Pond (Currie 1990b). The excavation of the main part of the garden was published in Currie & Locock (1993a). In tidying up work on the site, previous work by Peter Twigg was published (Locock & Currie 1991), plus a small trial excavation in the North Garden (Currie & Locock 1993b).

Castle Bromwich was a large walled garden covering four hectares, with a further designed landscape containing tree avenues extending into parkland beyond. When the site was described in 1575 it comprised the house, outhouses, orchards and gardens covering only one hectare (Locock 1993d, 165–66). By the early 18th century a number of formal walled compartments and terraces had formed around the house, but these were substantially enlarged under Sir John Bridgeman between c 1730 and 1747 until the walled areas extended to their present size. Bridgeman died with the works apparently still underway, but after his death the family moved their attentions to another of their properties at Weston Park (where they employed Capability Brown to design the landscape). The Castle Bromwich Hall gardens were neglected until *c* 1820 when renewed interest was taken in them. They continued to develop into the early 20th century, but fell into serious neglect after the Second World War (1939–45). When the Castle Bromwich Hall Gardens Trust was formed in the early 1980s to rescue them, many of the walls and garden buildings had become ruined and had been subjected to vandalism.

a) Excavation results

Archaeological evidence has shown that there has been horticultural activity at the site of Castle Bromwich Hall from the medieval period. Since the present Hall was begun (*c*. 1600), the gardens have been subject to many modifications of layout, style and usage.

Medieval cultivation

A medieval estate existed on the site from at least the 13th century, leaving layers of enriched soils containing large quantities of coarse medieval pottery. This could represent a general cultivation area close to a medieval house. Seed remains from a large medieval pit indicated a wide variety of crops were grown on the estate. These included all the common cereals, plus apple/pear and legumes.

Late Elizabethan/early Stuart garden c 1600–20

During this time the present hall was constructed, and the first identifiable garden was laid out in the area now known as the Best Garden. This garden design appears to have been terraced into at least two levels. A wall ran from east to west across this area. The upper terrace was the more complex, containing linear beds, together with planting pits for larger shrub-like plants. The latter were probably topiaried shrubs. There was evidence for manuring of the beds from the stables, leading to the introduction of cereal and bean seeds to the soil.

Formal gardens and parterres c 1680–1730

The Bridgeman family acquired Castle Bromwich in 1657 from the previous owners, the Devereux family. Sir John Bridgeman I (1631–1710) and Sir John Bridgeman II (1667–1747) both made significant contributions to the development of the gardens

The Best Garden underwent change during this period, with the lower terrace being brought up to the level of the upper terrace, and a new terrace being created to the west. This new design bore similarities to that shown on a print by Henry Beighton of 1726, although the archaeology revealed some discrepancies. The evidence suggested a garden *parterre* based on rectangular beds with linear gravel divisions between, forming what appeared to be a *parterre a l'anglais*. New walls were built around the upper terrace at this time that still survives today. A test trench in an area to the north of the house known as the North Garden revealed evidence for a *parterre* broadly similar to that shown on the Beighton print (Currie & Locock 1993b).

Expansion c 1730–47

This was a major period of construction, involving the building of the lower garden walls, the Orangery, and the Music Room. The middle terrace was laid out, although

Figure 39: Castle Bromwich Hall, West Midlands: a good example of an almost perfectly preserved formal mirror pond, dated to c 1740, under excavation. The pond was abandoned after 1747 and was then buried under a tennis court. Excavation recovered perfectly preserved clay walls, a clay lining and a brick and stone sluice at the end furthest from the camera.

only slight evidence of planting was found. Three ponds were made in the Slip Garden. The most elaborate was the apsidal-ended mirror pond, known as the West Pond (Currie 1990b), at the end of the Western Vista, but this appears to have been filled in by 1800. Environmental sampling revealed a well-managed garden that continued to be enhanced by manure from the stables. Pollen from holly and walnut recovered from soil samples were thought to represent plants grown in the garden during this period.

Neglect c 1747–1818
Following the death of Sir John Bridgeman II in 1747, the gardens went through a period of neglect. Those closest to the Hall had some maintenance from the tenants living there, but environmental sampling seemed to suggest neglect of the lower gardens. The *parterre* in the North Garden may have been destroyed before c 1780.

Renewed interest c 1818–1936
The Bridgemans began to show renewed interest in Castle Bromwich from c 1818, and work was begun reviving the gardens. New steps were built leading from the upper terrace to the lower gardens, and elsewhere the terraces were altered to present a less formal appearance. By this time the West Pond had been infilled. The Holly Walk was

Figure 40: Castle Bromwich Hall, West Midlands: this photograph of 1868 was discovered after the excavation of the Best Garden, but it clearly confirms the excavation results.

laid out as a terraced gravel walk significantly higher than the previous 18th-century level. There seems to have been a major planting programme on the Middle Terrace, creating the Upper Wilderness. In the 'Rose Garden' at the end of this terrace, a number of temporary beds, thought to be for nursery plants, were found.

Around the middle of the century the Maze seems to have been planted, and boilers were introduced to the Melon Ground.

The Best Garden underwent a number of changes culminating in a *parterre* design based on four Maltese crosses. These were set within a lawn with an internal design of flower beds between gravel areas. The beds within the Maltese crosses were circular, oval or triangular, forming a neat geometric pattern. This pattern was simplified on at least two occasions before 1940. Soon thereafter serious neglect set in.

b) Spatial analysis

An interesting exercise in interpreting a historic garden was attempted by Martin Locock using spatial analysis (Locock 1994). The methodology has been much used on historic buildings and settlement archaeology (Faulkner 1958, Hillier & Hanson 1985), but its use in gardens had not been published before Locock's effort, and this shows most clearly how gardens can be used to generate a whole new area of research. He applied a number of tests, including gamma analysis, to the gardens,[1] and was able to show that the initially perceived idea of a garden as a purely private space cannot be entirely supported. His provisional conclusion was that the formal garden was designed to give controlled access to a wide variety of persons ranging from servants, guests and strangers. The controller of this access was the owner, who allowed access to the garden at his discretion (Locock 1994, 248).

The confined nature of the walled gardens at Castle Bromwich may have provided a special set of access rules that might differ from the late informal gardens of the English Landscape Movement. One of the more interesting points about these gardens was their more open nature, and the increasing 'tourism' that grew up in this period. At Hagley Hall in the West Midlands, tourism was especially popular in the later 18th century, to such an extent that it rapidly became such a problem that the owners were forced to close the park to visitors in 1826, reversing their earlier policy of relatively open access (Currie 1998c, 199). A spatial survey of informal gardens could demonstrate different results that might considerable enhance our understanding of how these landscapes functioned, and how that changed over time.

c) Conclusions: the significance of the archaeological excavations at Castle Bromwich

As well as being the first garden excavation in the UK to be fully published (Kenyon *op cit*), the work at Castle Bromwich was also responsible for a number of other innovations in British garden archaeology. It was the first site in the UK to prove that sampling for historic seed and pollen on garden sites was worthwhile. As well as sampling for seed, the work at Castle Bromwich pioneered special soil sampling techniques, which showed that garden soils were frequently so enhanced that they seldom remained in their original state. Although such a statement might be obvious on hindsight, the academic world had not realised that enhancement created separate micro-environments within each plant bed designed to suit the plants grown therein. These 'altered soils' are often capable of preserving seed and/or pollen (Currie 1995a).

What made the publication of the Castle Bromwich report even more significant was that it was the first time that quantities of plant beds had been recovered by archaeological means. Before this, archaeological excavation had tended to concentrate on the recovery of foundations of 'hard structures' such as garden walls and summer houses. The general opinion before Castle Bromwich was that gardens were so dug over that plant beds were unlikely to survive. That Castle Bromwich overturned this negative thinking was, perhaps, the most significant aspect of the work. Subsequent excavations have continued to demonstrate the value of the techniques pioneered at Castle Bromwich, with environmental sampling and specialised soil analysis now well established as standard techniques in British garden excavations.

II) ROXFORD, HERTFORDSHIRE

The earthworks of a remarkable small garden containing many formal elements was brought to the attention of the public by the indefatigable efforts of Patience Bagenal, who lives in a cottage nearby (Bagenal 1994). The site is in a wood called Grotto Wood that is surrounded by gravel diggings that are now being used as a landfill site. In view of the uncertain future of the site the Hertfordshire Gardens Trust commissioned the author to make a measured survey of the remains. They are quite astonishing, compressing the remains of so many features typical of the formal garden into a single site less than a hectare in extent (Currie 2005).

The site is not completely symmetrical being an irregular shaped wood of roughly square dimensions, about 150m by 150m at its widest points, with a semi-circular projection at its southern end with a radius of about 45m. It stands approximately 1.5km. SSE of the village of Hertingfordbury, and 150m NW of Roxford Farm, centred on TL 301105. The latter is probably on the site of a sub-manor of Hertingfordbury mentioned in Domesday Book. There are traces of a homestead moat here alongside the River Lea. Grotto Wood stands on the edge of a gravel plateau some 20m above the valley bottom at a height of about 61m AOD at the southern end of the wood, rising to 69.5m in the north-west corner.

Around 1660 the sub-manor of Roxford had passed to George Chalncombe. His widow conveyed the property to John Brassey in 1700. The Brassey family continued to hold the manor until 1801, when they sold it to William Baker of Bayfordbury. Research by Patience Bagenal has uncovered previously unknown material about the earthworks in Grotto Wood, including a lengthy description by Richard Dick, dated between 1739 and 1765, and a poem by Thomas Green dated 1775. The site first appears on Drury and Andrews' Topographical Map of Hertfordshire of 1766, as an elaborate garden in the formal style that corresponds roughly with the shape of the present garden remains. By 1789 the garden had been destroyed by an Alderman Kirby, who had removed all the structural materials for reuse. Shortly afterwards it was planted as a wood.

At the high end of the site was a large spiral mount, which contained a cave at the bottom and a summer house at the top. The mount was approached by a raised gravel walk running along the west side of the wood. Below the mount was an aviary at the head of the first pond, a linear canal. At the end of this was an octagonal basin with an island in the middle that once held a statue of Neptune. The basin also contained a fountain on one side. Below the basin was another linear pond and at the far end of this was a grotto and cold bath. Both ponds and grotto were much adorned with shellwork and flints, but there is no sign of these today. The aviary has gone, and all that is left are the earthworks of the spiral mount, the three ponds, and a crescent-shaped mound where the grotto once stood. The gravel walk survives along the west side, and there are traces of further banks around the other sides of the wood, suggesting the limits of the garden.

The measured survey was based on a rectangular grid laid out by manual theodolite in 1994–95. The work was much hampered by the overgrown nature of the wood, and aid was received by a small band of volunteers from the Hertfordshire Gardens Trust, who cut a number of transects through the thick cover of brambles so that tapes could be stretched across the site. The difficulties encountered prevented a contour survey from being completed, but individual levels were inserted on the archive plan. The author had to travel some three kilometers across the excavated gravel workings to reach the nearest OS bench mark. Although the outline of the wood hinted that the site was not completely symmetrical, it was only after the survey had been completed that the true nature of this irregularity showed up. The only plan of the site was the drawing shown on Andrews and Drury's map of 1766, and this seemed to show it as a rectangle with apsidal ends to the north and south. The regularity shown on the map proved to be false (*ibid*).

The mystery of this site was that it was not within clear site of any house, but stood alone, apparently without any obvious designed landscape between it and the nearest house, Roxford Manor. It stood within land owned by the Manor, but the siting of this unusual formal garden is odd. Gardens hidden from the house are known[2], but in the formal garden period under discussion they tended to complement the architecture of the house, and to do so had to be in contact with that architecture. A further curiosity was that the garden seemed to be admired at a time (1775) when formal landscapes were generally despised. It may be that the cave and the grotto were such exceptional examples of their kind that they could be admired even if the general style of the garden was unfashionable. Sybil Wade, the landscape architect who worked with the author on the project, suggested that elements of the garden may have been perceived as more rococo than formal, and were hence considered fashionable for longer than if the garden had been seen purely as a formal design (pers comm).

Following the measured survey, further funds were found to make management recommendations for the site. This included taking cored samples from the silts of the pond, in the hope that they might give some further information on the site. These were found to be largely contaminated, and were of little use. This could have been predicted, as silt only tends to build up in historic ponds after they have been abandoned.

(See end of Section for notes)

Chapter 12: The informal designed landscape

I) GENERAL CONSIDERATIONS

The informal garden has often been considered difficult terrain for archaeologists by garden historians. The unpredictability of these designs, most popular in the UK between about 1740 and 1820, makes it initially harder to locate its irregular features, but, given patience, and good preliminary research, the unpredictable can become predictable after a fashion, and garden archaeology has been successful on this type of site. The sites chosen as case studies for this book are The Leasowes in the West Midlands and Leigh Park in Hampshire. The former is one of the earliest 'true' informal designs, and one of the rare examples that were not designed by a professional. Leigh Park is a relatively late example of an 'English Landscape Garden', being largely created after 1820 by Sir George Staunton, who had travelled much in China.

The main problem with informal gardens is what to target. Often the plan defies any rigid system that can be predicted. The irregular nature of the layout prevents the systematic scheme of trial trenches that can be useful in formal gardens being applied so readily here. Many past projects involving informal designs have tended to target specific features, rather than to use archaeology to determine the overall plan. Certainly area excavation tends to be limited to specific areas as the overall size of most informal gardens is prohibitive. Many of Brown or Repton's designs exceed 300 hectares, and even with the largest budgets available to archaeology, only a small percentage of such areas can be examined.

For this reason the implementation of a thorough cartographic and landscape survey of the site is a prime requisite before any archaeology is undertaken. Although all archaeological sites should undergo such analysis, where possible, it is of particular importance on these sites. Only once this work has been undertaken will it be possible to determine which areas require below ground excavation.

Most projects working on these sites tend to target buildings. These were often the main focal points of this type of design, the planting being set out as a backdrop to such buildings or being arranged in such a way as to offer the best views to and from them. Over the years the site where the most detailed work of this sort has been carried out is at Stowe, Buckinghamshire, where there are probably more garden buildings, both surviving and vanished, than any other garden in the UK. As every year passes, the National Trust's annual reports give summary details of works on yet another structure within this complex landscape (eg Marshall 2002).

So varied are these gardens that it is not possible to lay down a general strategy for them as a whole. It is considered that the best way to approach these is by giving two examples from sites known first hand to the author.

II) LEIGH PARK

This site was excavated in 1992 (Currie 1995b). The estate covered about 400 hectares when it was sold to Sir George Staunton in 1820, and was further extended by him.

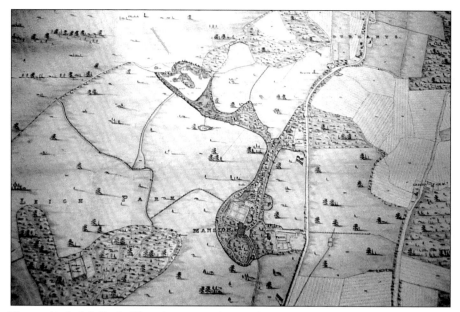

Figure 41: Leigh Park (Hants): a map of 1842 shows Sir George Staunton's elaborate designed landscape, a great aid to the excavations.

Today the site is divided by a modern road and has a large post-war housing estate extending to its southern and eastern boundaries. It was originally thought that Staunton was responsible for creating it, but research has shown that much of the Pleasure Grounds had already been laid out by Staunton's predecessor, William Garrett, who had owned the estate between 1800 and 1819.

The estate began as small villa with a walled garden and a few paddocks of about four hectares, purchased by William Garrett from the widow of a retired naval officer in 1800. In 1802 Garrett considerably extended the property by purchasing the adjoining farm together with about 100 hectares of land. From hereon he was able to begin designing a country house estate in the then-prevalent 'English Landscape Garden' tradition. The farm was converted to a Regency *ferme ornée*, a popular feature of contemporary country house estates, and the mansion house rebuilt in a fashionable style with an octagonal Gothic library attached. By the time George Staunton died in 1859 the landscape comprised an extensive mix of features and styles. Around the house, and beyond, the design contained a number of thematic areas based on different countries around the world. Thus to the west of the house was an 'American' garden, and to the SE a 'Dutch' garden with a Swiss cottage beyond. The apex of the design contained a lake, and it was here that Staunton tried to incorporate as many different 'national' styles as possible. Thus the ornamental features around the lake contained a Chinese fort, a Corinthian bridge, and a Turkish tent, as well as other items of whimsy such as a Shell House, a Greek Temple, a 'rural cottage' and a monument to Lord Canning. The lake itself had many similarities to that at Stourhead, Wiltshire, and the large number of buildings showed the influence of

Stowe, particularly Staunton's 'Temple' which had tablets inscribed with memorial to friends and relatives reminiscent of Stowe's earlier 'Temple of British Worthies'.

The brief for the work at Leigh was to 'locate the paths and basic layout of the Staunton landscape'. It was the paths that often marked out the means of circulation around the garden. For the most part these had been lost. Detailed maps of the site at various stages of its history enabled most of the lost buildings to be located. There were too many to explore them all so the excavations concentrated on trying to recover an idea of what some of the more important lost garden structures looked like. No formal written brief existed, and the project evolved in a rather *ad hoc* manner with the author often suggesting the most effective ways to spend the allocated budget. In the end 26 trenches were excavated. Most of these were linear test trenches seeking to locate lost features. Once located the trenches were sometimes expanded.

In the case of the Dutch Garden, a garden building was discovered that did not appear to be shown on any of the detailed contemporary plans of the site. It did not display any characteristics of 'Dutch' design and may have been an earlier feature sited because of its ability to obtain good views over the Solent to the south. The Dutch garden, which did not appear to have the elements of formality expected from such a design, may have been laid out in front of this building to act as a 'foreground' to the view. In the Farmhouse Garden, a shrub-based planting design typical of the Regency informal style was encountered.

Figure 42: Leigh Park, Hants: the excavation of a flint and timber garden structure in the Dutch Garden not obviously shown on any of the site's numerous contemporary plans. Proof that even on sites that have the best documentary and cartographic records, the unexpected can still be found during excavation. Tim Allen and Rob Atkins undertake the excavation.

The garden paths were often of a robust nature that had survived relatively intact beneath later grass covering. Once the general area had been located from historic plans, many were located by simple probing with surveyor's arrows. Thick layers of well-compacted gravel formed most of the paths. In the case of the central path in the walled garden (possibly the oldest path on the site, dating from the late 18th century), the gravel was set in an excavated trench and was over 300mm deep. On retrospect, it is considered that such was the solid nature of many of them that they would probably have made good targets for a geophysical survey. Unfortunately the overall area of the site was too large to commission this sort of work. Besides, the methods used to identify path location were sufficient to recover the information required and were cheaper. All the targeted paths were found by the simple methods indicated above. However, not all sites will have such good cartographic sources as Leigh Park, and in almost every case there the remains of both paths and structures existed below only a thin covering of turf. Few of the trenches excavated needed to be deeper than 400mm. This leads on to what is often the most surprising aspect of garden archaeology: the ability of relatively ephemeral features to survive close to the surface. This was noted at formal gardens such as Castle Bromwich, and was to appear again at The Leasowes, the other informal site destined for discussion here.

III) THE LEASOWES

The Leasowes is a large public park within the West Midlands conurbation, being part of Dudley Metropolitan Borough. It is surrounded entirely by housing and industry. The open areas of the park are mainly managed as a golf course. There are two main streams that empty into the Priory Pool. The stream valleys are wooded for the most part, and have a number of smaller ponds along their line.

The park was laid out as a designed landscape in the English Landscape style by the poet, William Shenstone, between 1743 and 1763. Prior to this it had been farmland, and little has been recorded of its pre-18th-century archaeology or history. Shenstone ornamented the natural landscape by building artificial ponds, cascades and follies, including a mock medieval 'priory' ruin. He also improved the views and vistas by judicious planting. Under Shenstone, the site gained much popular renown, and was considered to have had much influence on later 18th-century landscape design. This continued after Shenstone's death in 1763, but the encroachment of urbanisation on its views and vistas in the 19th century led to its slow decline. Despite the removal of nearly all of Shenstone's ornamental features, the overall landscape has survived reasonably well (Gallagher 1996).

The site has suffered from ravages common to public parks in urban areas. There has been some vandalism, and the area suffers from litter and the unstructured use by dog-walkers. The presence of the golf course frequently conflicts with the original ethos of the landscape by introducing large earthworks (bunkers) into the park, and removing features that were part of the original design. Until recently, management of the golf course had been undertaken without consideration being given to the historic landscape, although the stream valleys have been largely unaffected. However, the features along these have been much neglected. Ponds have become silted or dewatered through breaches of the dams. Cascades have become much altered and ruinous, and everywhere have become covered in silt, years of decaying leaves, and rank undergrowth.

The Leasowes was an unusual site to work on as the requirements of the work were very specific, rather than a study of the entire landscape. For the latter the reader is referred to Gallagher (*ibid*). These requirements included an unusual survey of a considerable length of stream bed covering some 1000m between existing ponds. As well as mapping earthworks along this stream, a collection of masonry debris in the stream bed was made. This was done in the hope of identifying concentrations of older materials, and thus the location of some of Shenstone's ornamental features. This exercise was, to all intents, carried out as a 'field walk' of the stream, in which building materials were collected from designated sections and weighed, counted and analysed. Initial inspection of the streams suggested that this exercise would not produce any worthwhile results, particularly as the streams seemed to be littered with recently dumped modern debris. The latter did prove to be the case, but the 'field walk' also produced some interesting and unexpected results.

As initially thought there was little survival of building materials from Shenstone's era and the streams were littered with modern debris from its time as a municipal park. Taken at face value it might have been considered that the author wasted valuable time and resources undertaking this work,[3] but analysis showed quite the opposite. The remarkable conclusion to this unusual piece of work was that the modern materials seemed to be most highly concentrated near to where it was thought Shenstone had erected his more substantial features. This was usually immediately below pond dams, and on the site of the numerous cascades. By contrast the older bricks likely to have been from Shenstone's era survived in only small numbers, but tended to be found well away from where his features were thought to be! The conclusion was not that Shenstone's features had been wrongly located by later commentators, but that they had become ruinous, and when the municipal authorities took over the site at the beginning of the 20th century they cleared away all the debris around the features. They then appear to have attempted rebuilding some of the features, but with very little regard to what was there originally. So, whereas Shenstone would possibly have taken advantage of a pond dam to build a rustic cascade where the water exited, the municipal authorities built a purely utilitarian, workmanlike sluice or spillway. The life expectancy of such features, even when built of concrete and engineering bricks, is generally short if not regularly maintained because of the highly erosive nature of streams. Consequently these 'new' features quickly became ruinous and fell down leaving masses of debris in the stream immediately below where they had been.

The reason why Shenstonian materials only survived well away from his features was that these areas were neglected by the municipal renovations, They had got there, in small quantities, through flood action, and were left there undisturbed, giving a somewhat inverted impression of Shenstone's activity. If this exercise had not been carried out, it would be tempting to believe that the failure to find Shenstonian features in the stream was the result of them being wrongly located. This might have led to further money being expended trying to find them, a mainly hopeless task as the 'field walk' had demonstrated that the features had been largely destroyed by the unrecorded municipal 'tidying up' in the early 20th century. This is a shame because it is likely that many of Shenstone's cascades would have looked like a random pile of stones to the untrained eye of the early 20th-century municipal operative.[4]

Figure 43: The Leasowes, West Midlands: John Hutchinson, Dr Neil Rushton and Trevor Steptoe excavating the remains of the Priory Cottage, William Shenstone's much admired 18th-century gothic folly.

One of the best known of Shenstone's ornamental features was the Priory Cottage. This was a relatively early example of introducing a Gothic 'folly' into the landscape. The cottage had been demolished at the beginning of the 20th century and its remains buried under a golf tee. However, a good portion of it survived in woodland adjoining. Again, like on so many garden sites, the remains were relatively well preserved very close to the surface, and the only serious damage to them had been caused by tree roots. Where the excavation butted against the edge of the golf tee, it seems that the walls had survived to even greater heights, and it is possible that survival underneath is very good.

The excavation of the Priory Cottage demonstrated the highly contrived nature of such features. It appears that it was only on the side from which the cottage was viewed that it appeared as a Gothic folly with pointed windows etc, imitating a ruined abbey. Behind this façade it was a brick cottage, with Shenstone and subsequent owners of the estate obtaining rent from the tenant who lived therein (Ponsford 2000, 306–07). Around the British countryside there are many examples of 'follies' that actually hide similar utilitarian use.

A landscape similar to The Leasowes can be seen at Painshill, Surrey. This was also built by a dilettante owner, Charles Hamilton (1704–86). It was an elaborate landscape full of architectural follies set around the focal point of a large serpentine lake and laid out between 1738 and 1773. The site is currently owned by the Painshill Park Trust, which has saved the site from years of neglect. The idea of erecting follies and views based around a lake has been much repeated as can be seen at Leigh Park. Hamilton's buildings included a Gothic Temple, an elaborate bridge, Mausoleum, Temple of

111

Bacchus, Grotto and Turkish Tent. Many of these features had to be recovered by archaeological excavation, and the buildings on their sites today are reconstructions (Howes 1991; Collier & Wrightson 1993). Much of the work here was based on archaeological excavations undertaken by Lesley Howes in the1980s. Again the nature of the design led to the archaeological methodology being based largely on the recovery of structures, in this instance for the purposes of reconstruction. The result of this work is open to public inspection most days of the year.

Although Howes (1991, 74) refers to efforts made at Painshill to recover information about non-structural elements, such as paths, at the time of writing nothing concerning this aspect of the project has been published. It is only at Leigh Park that a non-structural approach based largely on the recovery of paths and associated planting was undertaken, and the work subsequently published. It is easy to understand why such an approach is seldom published, the catalogue of paths recorded at Leigh Park (Currie 1995b) hardly constitutes an interesting read to the non-specialist![6] Nevertheless, it needs to be stressed that such information is highly useful to understanding how one circulated around such a garden, and how the various structures were interlinked with one another.

(See end of Section for notes)

Chapter 13: Water gardens

Water gardens are a distinct type of garden that have been popular throughout history. Today some garden centres specialise solely in providing items for water gardens. The term water garden can sometimes be ambiguous. Some people give the term to sites where water features are only one element within a garden layout, and it is possible that it can be applied too freely. It is rare that historical commentators used the term, preferring to comment on water features as if they were part of a greater whole. Despite this the term is common with garden historians. This author has done work at a number of sites that might be termed water gardens. The definition he would prefer is where water is the main element of the garden design. Such gardens would appear to be relatively spartan in other elements, particularly in plant–orientated designs, although trees, in the form of avenues, clumps and belts are often elements of such gardens.

This chapter looks at two gardens that had water as their apparent principal element: Court of Noke, Hereford, and Upper Lodge in Bushy Park, Greater London. It also looks at the work on a large water feature that was a major element in a larger designed landscape, the formal cascade at The Gnoll, Neath, South Wales.

I) COURT OF NOKE

The work at Court of Noke involved two phases, a desk-based assessment of the history of the site, followed by a watching brief on the reinstatement of the canal-like features around two sides of the house (Currie & Rushton 2001). The historical research revealed an unusual history. It would appear that the present house was built towards the end of the 17th century by a well-to-do merchant who retired to the country. The house was, therefore, not a true aristocratic mansion, but a middling sort of property, whose gardens are seldom very elaborate when compared with those of more wealthy landowners. Such sites received little attention before the 1990s, the majority of garden research being directed by an art historical approach at the more elaborate gardens of the very rich. The male line of the family failed within sixty years of the garden's creation, and the house declined to the status of farm. By the early 19th century the water features were being used to power an animal feed mill on the side of one of the farm buildings, and many of the garden features seem to have disappeared.

Initially the water features on the site seemed to be little more than a system of linear ponds that can be commonly found at medieval and early post-medieval sites throughout England and lowland Wales from wealthy yeoman status upwards. It was only during the dredging of the ponds that their ornamental nature became fully appreciated. Much of the work was done before the dredging proper took place as many of the features were revealed once the ponds were drained down. The archaeological work at Court of Noke involved very little real digging. The ponds/canals were simply drained down, and the features largely revealed themselves in the silt. Much of the latter drained away when the ponds were emptied, although some hand cleaning and minor trenching was required. There have been a number of instances where the author has been able to record otherwise unsuspected features simply through being present when ponds or moats were drained down. For example old wooden pipes and a fine timber sluice was recorded when the moat and associated fishponds were drained down at Baddesley Clinton, Warwickshire (Currie 1994b, 2000b). A similar wooden pipe to those found at this site was found at Noke connecting two of the ponds.

The final 'pond' nearest the house turned out to be particularly interesting. This was revealed as a T-shaped canal that contained a small island at the end of one arm on which sat a stone summer house or similar shelter from which it was possible to look along the pond towards a substantial wooden bridge, with a stone sluice at the far end. The stonework around the sluice seemed too elaborate for simple utilitarian use, and it is possible that some ornamental structure existed there. In the other arm of the 'T', which was parallel to the main front of the house, the canal was found to be lined by cobbles, and to be revetted in timber. In the centre of this arm were two equidistant brick bases that seemed to be designed to support statues rising out of the canal, and standing symmetrically opposite the main windows of the house. Behind the statues was an area of further structural remains whose purpose was unknown, but seemed to be further ornamentation related to the statues.

There was no real evidence of other garden features within the area defined by the ponds. There was a small partly walled area at the back of the house that was probably a kitchen garden, and beyond was evidence for an orchard, a common component of Herefordshire gardens. In front of the house was a lawn bounded by the T-shaped canal. There was no suggestion that there had been anything more substantial here, although archaeological excavation may one day reveal a small *parterre*. It would seem, therefore, that the principal method of ornamentation for this house was the

Figure 44: Court of Noke, Hereford: The T-shaped canal during the refilling ceremony, following dredging

water features. Although the two more distant 'ponds' were probably simple linear canals, the T-shaped canal by the house and its associated features must have been quite impressive.

The lesson to be learnt from this exercise is that a lot can be learnt from watching water features being drained down. Important information was obtained about this site, and our knowledge of the ornamentation of the houses of the lesser gentry in the period 1670–1740 was greatly increased for a relatively modest cost.

II) UPPER LODGE, BUSHY PARK

The excavations at Upper Lodge were far more elaborate, and had a much larger budget. The results were published in *Post-Medieval Archaeology* (Currie *et* al 2003). Bushy Park was attached to Hampton Court shortly after the Dissolution, and Upper Lodge became one of two important lodges sited therein. Research by Cathy White and the late Peter Foster revealed that between 1709 and 1715 the Earl of Halifax obtained a long lease of the this site from the Crown, and proceeded to lay out extensive water features to ornament the rebuilt house. These included lengthy canals, numerous basins, and a cascade with attendant grottoes. The cascade was much praised by contemporaries, and was the subject of a number of contemporary illustrations, one of which is contained in the Royal Collection.

The research by White and Foster prompted a Lottery Fund bid to restore the water gardens. Although this bid ultimately failed, it attracted much interest, and subsequent funding for the archaeological work came from a number of sources. This found that Halifax was not the first tenant of the lodge to undertake ornamental landscaping. Excavation near the site of the early house revealed a series of walled compartments, with elaborate brick piers. A plan of the site made just before Halifax's tenure showed the house to be at the centre of a series of extensive tree avenues.

Halifax diverted the Longford River through the park to create a canal leading into an oval basin. From here a neat cascade, flanked by shellwork grottoes, tumbled into a lower basin. Between this and another basin some distance to the east was a raised terrace extended some few hundred metres across the front of the house. Walks perambulated this extensive terrace, with an oval 'central' basin in front of the house. At the east end of the terrace was another basin, followed by a long length of linear canal connecting it to yet another basin, and a further length of canal. In total the length of canals, terrace and basins extended over 900m making it one of the most extensive systems in the country at the time.

It terms of display, the water features at Upper Lodge were relatively simple. The cascade had a mere six steps, and paled in comparison to the roughly contemporary cascades at The Gnoll, Glamorgan, Six Oaks in Nottinghamshire and Chatsworth in Derbyshire. Despite this, it was one of the best known examples of its kind in the country in its day, and one of the few UK sites cited as an example of good taste in the contemporary work on water features by Stephen Switzer (1729).

Excavation at Upper Lodge comprised largely a series of evaluations, funded first by the Lottery Fund, and, then by subsequent developers and the Crown Estate, who took over a much reduced scheme to restore the setting of Upper Lodge. These found the site much disturbed, particularly during the site's long tenure by the Ministry of Defence, and good archaeological survival was highly localised. Many areas proved to

Figure 45: Upper Lodge, Bushy Park: the remains of Lord Halifax's much-admired early 18th-century cascade.

be almost completely devoid of archaeology. It was largely the perseverance of local parties, supported by English Heritage, which extracted funds for continued work on the site.

The main focus of the work was to recover the form of the Central Basin in front of the house. This found only fragmentary evidence for this basin, and if it were not for the clear cartographic evidence that it existed, it is doubtful whether the archaeology could have recognised what the heavily disturbed remains represented. Preliminary strip evaluation trenches recovered the remains of a 19th-century concrete fountain on the site of the basin, plus earlier walls and conduits, but no clear evidence for the basin itself. More extensive excavations a few years later revealed more of the walls, showing them to have been a series of walled compartments, and a extensive system of drains, but no obvious basin. It was concluded that the basin had been levelled when the area was informalised in the later 18th century.

Initially it seemed that evaluation trenches in the vicinity of the cascade would not be fruitful. This feature seemed to be much rebuilt in the 20th century, and it was only through careful observation that elements of the original design began to become obvious. Despite extensive earthmoving in the 19th century that destroyed the original shape of the lower pond, and covered the site with much contemporary rubbish, the footprint of one of the grottoes flanking the cascade had survived. Provisionally this seemed to be no more than a fragment of the original feature, two stub walls extending a mere 0.5m from the revetment wall that existed either side of the cascade. It was only on reference to a contemporary description that it was realised that this shallow alcove was all that had ever existed. A letter written by Samuel Molyneux in February 1714 explains how this deceit had been contrived:

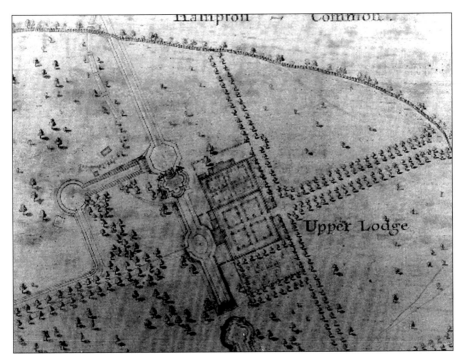

Figure 46: A plan of Upper Lodge dated c 1735, showing Lord Halifax's water gardens (PRO MR 1454).

From Hampton Court we went to... Bushy Park...there was here little or nothing remarkable but the Cascade which was not very high, but little and yet very beautifully dispos'd so as to fall between two fine pieces of Grotto Work where are places left for Paintings representing two Caves in which little walks around the Basin of the Cascade end the Paintings are moveable so as to be taken away in Winter (Hunt & Willis 1989, 148–9).

Further remains at the back of the revetment wall showed supporting masonry for the domes that covered the grottoes. Other features that were identified only after careful examination of historical sources included the remains of water spouts and a stone basin set into the revetment wall.

Although evidence for the pre-Halifax site was relatively easy to interpret, the remains of the water garden were more problematic. Extensive later disturbance left only fragmentary remains, and it is unlikely that they would have been clearly interpreted if not for the excellent contemporary plans and illustrations that survived, and had been extracted, often from obscure sources, by the researches of Cathy White and Peter Foster. The lesson to be learnt from Upper Lodge was that even when the archaeology is fragmentary, coordination with good local historians can produce excellent results worthy of publication in a national journal.

III) THE GNOLL, GLAMORGAN

The formal cascade at The Gnoll, is probably the largest feature of its kind to have been subjected to archaeological examination. Its subsequent publication was the icing on the cake of an interesting project (Currie *et al* 1994). This stone-lined cascade is several hundred metres in length falling over 20 metres into a large dammed pond known as The Fishpond. It was constructed in the 1720s by the Mackworth family to be seen on the opposite side of the valley from the site of the house. It must have taken great effort to construct, but it never seemed to work properly. It seems that the water supply system was modified and expanded on a number of occasions in the following years, before finally being abandoned, possibly as early as the 1740s. Around this time, the Mackworths created a more fashionable 'informal' cascade elsewhere in the park. They seemed to have learnt their lesson in the failure of the first cascade to work properly because the later work still operates today.

The remains of the formal canal were gradually covered over by eroding soil, undergrowth and leaf litter until the early 1990s when a community project began uncovering the remains. This had progressed to a considerable extent with quantities of covering earth being removed before the significance of the discovery was recognised. It was only at this late stage that archaeologists were called in to make a measured survey and interpretation of the highly complex remains. Very little excavation was required, and this project involved largely a measured survey of the structural remains and the associated earthworks. The end result was as instructive as anyone could have hoped, and the publication was able to modify previous views on historical cascades in the UK. On retrospect, it might be possible to argue that it was a shame archaeologists were not called in earlier, and that the earth covering the feature might have revealed more information if removed under archaeological supervision. Judging from what was seen this may not have provided much more additional information, and the resultant measured survey was able, with the aid of documentary sources, to date the feature to within a few years, and it seems unlikely that much else concerning the complex water management necessary to run the feature could have been gained that was not obtained from this survey work.

The feature was too large to record on a stone by stone basis. Instead a block plan approach was followed, with more detailed recording where the remains merited it. Despite the overall formal outer edges of the main cascade, the steps along its length were not of an even width and size, such as at the smaller Upper Lodge cascade described above. Steps in the Gnoll cascade varied in height and length so that the overall fall of water was broken up into different forms of display.

At the head of the cascade was a large earthen bank with an arch within it through which the water fell. Above this bank, and partly concealed by it, were the mechanisms that allowed the cascade to function. It is possible that there were three different phases here, each one apparently executed to try to bring more water to the head of the cascade. The initial water supply seems to have been a well-head fed by a small stream. To supplement this two larger streams were diverted and brought to the head of the cascade by way of a substantial embanked leat. Finally the Mackworths seem to have constructed a reserve reservoir above the cascade. It would seem that this reserve was only released to provide an extra, short-term, rush of water, possibly when the owner wanted to impress an important guest. This would have probably required careful timing, with a gardener opening a sluice at a given signal. It is uncertain if these changes were carried out in rapid sequence as it was found that each previous change had failed to provide enough water, or if a number of years passed between each phase. Whatever the case, it seems that the cascade had an overall short life, and was probably abandoned within about 20–30 years of construction.

Looking back on this project, it was not the measured survey of the stone structure of the cascade that enabled its workings to be established, but a wider topographical survey that identified the supply leats. This confirms the importance when dealing with water features of understanding how the water would have been supplied. As stated in the chapter on survey, a study of the changes of level is an essential requirement.

It is ironic that within a few years of reconstruction the cascade seems to have encountered difficulties in getting a sufficient head of water along it to turn it into a worthwhile spectacle. It would seem that the historic problems that appear to have led to its abandonment have resurfaced in the present.

(See end of Section for notes)

Chapter 14: Town gardens

Town gardens can be defined as relatively small gardens attached to town houses in a confined space. Such gardens seldom exceed a quarter of a hectare, and are rarely examined by archaeology, often because other elements of the site's archaeology take precedence. A trawl through published excavation reports on town house sites will often find gardens only mentioned in passing. This neglect may be changing now that garden archaeology is becoming increasingly recognised. However, what can be considered as a published excavation has only been undertaken on one town garden. This was undertaken between 1984 and 1986 at no 4, The Circus, Bath, by Robert Bell of the Bath Archaeological Trust, and subsequently published in *Garden History* (Bell 1990).

Like many archaeological projects, the work on this site was preceded by an evaluation. This discovered that the original garden had survived well to about 0.4m below the existing ground. Subsequent work proved this to be a roughly formal garden laid out in the 1760s when one might expect more informal design to be fashionable. This formality was reinforced by linear beds running along the two long edges of the garden that became progressively wider towards the far end. This gave the illusion that the garden plot was more rectangular than it actually was (*ibid*, 13).

Another unexpected characteristic of this garden was that the simple design (three oval plant beds) was set in a hard standing of compacted gravel that had been deliberately introduced. The excavators were surprised that the setting for the flower beds was not a lawn. This design remained largely unchanged until 1836/37 when a thick layer of new soil was dumped over the entire garden and a new design created (*op cit*, 14). It was this dumping that enabled the earlier garden to survive largely intact. This was another surprise to the archaeologists because it had been anticipated that subsequent garden features would have destroyed all trace of the earliest garden (Bell 1990, 20).

In 1995 a watching brief on drainage works next door at no 6 The Circus revealed similar survival in the garden, with a 1760s garden covered by a dump of earth before a new garden was laid out in the early 19th century (Ponsford & Jackson 1996, 255).

Many of the lessons learnt from The Circus have informed later garden excavations. The unusual discovery of plants beds set out in gravel, as opposed to lawn, was repeated at Castle Bromwich in successive phases. Also repeated at Castle Bromwich and elsewhere was the discovery that gardeners found it easier to dump new soils and begin again when designing new gardens on old sites. We are so used to the idea of digging through an older design that we assumed our preferences would have been carried out in historic times. The use of compacted gravel as the setting for the design clearly made digging through the old design hard work, and gardeners seem to have preferred the easier option of importing new soil and starting again when it was practical.

In his conclusions on The Circus, Bell asked if these two unusual features that he found might 'have occurred more frequently than has been appreciated, and there may be many other gardens which survive in an equally good condition' (*ibid*). He may not have realised how true his words were about to prove. As the presses were printing his article, so the excavations at Castle Bromwich were about to show his words prophetic. When one considers that The Circus was excavated less than 20 years ago, it

Figure 47: The Circus, Bath under excavation (Copyright Rob Bell)

has to be recognised what a milestone this work has proven to be, and how far we have advanced in such a short time.

At the time Bell excavated The Circus he was able to state that 'there was no precedent for the excavation of a town garden' (*op cit*, 1). This situation has changed very little since, although there have been numerous developer-led evaluations and watching briefs that have occurred in town garden areas. It is remarkable how few seem to have recorded garden features. It is possible that some of this stems from a want of looking, the garden features tending to be post-medieval have been machined away without examination in the desire to get down to older levels. This is frequently reflected in the aim of the brief which is often to explore the medieval archaeology. Although this could be the case in some instances, the author earns his everyday living excavating run-of-the-mill developer sites, and garden features are seldom recognised in town gardens even when one has an interest in locating them.

An exception was the elaborate garden urn fragments recently discovered in a late pit at the rear of 16–17 North Cross Street in Gosport, Hants (see Fig 37). The garden archaeology had been completely destroyed, but this find clearly showed that there had been town gardens in Gosport that had been of some elaboration. Gosport was a small port opposite Portsmouth where naval officers frequently had dwellings. Although not as fashionable as Bath in the 18th century, it would have had a certain air of refinement in the later 17th or early 18th century. A plan of the town dating to the late 17th century shows large backland areas. This plan shows no detail of the gardens, but such was the open area behind the houses, that small gardens of comparable size to The Circus in Bath would have been possible. By the 19th century the town had declined, and the backland areas built over with outbuildings and industrial structures. So tightly packed were these later structures that the surviving garden area behind 16–17 North Cross Street was barely 15 square metres in extent. Yet within a 19th-century pit was a remarkable fragment of a highly ornate horticultural urn (Ponsford 2004, in press) that hinted of a time when there may have been gardens similar to those at The Circus.

(See end of Section for notes)

Chapter 15: the Scottish experience

By Chris Currie and Robin Turner

It is possible to suggest that modern garden archaeology in the UK began in Scotland when Neil Hynd and Gordon Ewart examined the gardens of Aberdour Castle, Fife using archaeological techniques between 1977 and 1980 (Hynd & Ewart 1983). This resulted in an early example of a garden restoration that had been informed by archaeology. Gordon Ewart went on to influence garden archaeology outside Scotland, including Castle Bromwich in the West Midlands, where his foresight was partly responsible for inaugurating the extensive testing of archaeological methods with regard to their application in historic gardens. His encouragement of this work contributed to the present more enlightened attitude towards archaeology on European garden sites.

An overview of the state of archaeology in Scotland published in 1991 (Cruft 1991) showed that Hynd and Ewart's work at Aberdour remained the only garden site in Scotland to have received significant excavation up until that time, although as the case study in this chapter illustrates, this situation has changed significantly since the early 1990s.[7] Despite this recent increase and diversification of garden archaeology in Scotland, the case study of Aberdour remains useful.

The excavations at Aberdour recovered a series of terraces shown on a plan of 1740, the revetment walls that had held the terraces back against the steep hillside having survived to heights of between 350mm and 650mm, with a further 450mm of foundations below the original garden level (Hynd & Ewart 1983, 97). Unfortunately no evidence was found for any features within the garden that could be attributed to plant beds or other horticultural features. To compensate for this, soil samples were taken for pollen analysis in the hope of obtaining clues as to the type of planting undertaken (*ibid*, 105). Cruft (1991, 185) declared that this was 'disappointing with traces of contemporary plant material totally wanting'. However, this was a negative interpretation, and on retrospect there were some indications that the sampling was not quite as hopeless as this source indicates. Hynd and Ewart recorded pollen derived from mulberry and horse chestnut for which there was no obvious source from the modern area (Hynd & Ewart 1983, 105).

The work at Aberdour was undertaken when garden archaeology was in its infancy and although it seemed disappointing at the time, there were indications of the better things to come. In retrospect, the type of long narrow terraces excavated may have been no more than grassed landscape features – planted with occasional shrubs or ornamented with plants in large movable pots. This could account for the lack of horticultural features, an explanation supported by similar evidence from Castle Bromwich and elsewhere. More recent work at Aberdour Castle in the late 1990s, in the walled garden and on the primary terraces, found some evidence for plant beds (Ponsford 2000, 346), suggesting that the earlier results were a matter of trench location rather than archaeological method.

Many of Scotland's earliest gardens were attached to tower houses or other kinds of fortified residences, and were often restricted in size. From the 17th century, as

Scotland became more peaceful, largely as a result of James VI's accession to the English throne in 1603, many existing gardens were enlarged. Following the Restoration of Charles II in 1660, the way was opened for the development of great formal gardens in Scotland as at Glamis, Angus, Yester, East Lothian, and Holyroodhouse, Edinburgh – the latter the scene of recent archaeological work. Although many of these gardens have subsequently been swept away, the skeletons of some early designs still survive where the houses were deserted or abandoned for a time (Cruft 1991, 175–6), as is demonstrated at Aberdour Castle. At this latter site, the Earls of Morton allowed the castle to fall into disrepair when a new house was built south of Aberdour village, and the ruins were taken into Guardianship in 1924 (*ibid*, 185).

There are many parallels between Scottish gardens and those in the more upland areas of England and Wales.[8] Perhaps one of the most obvious characteristics of many Scottish gardens was the more rugged typography that designers had to deal with when laying out the types of design so popular in lowland areas of western Europe. Creating large areas of flat *parterres* was more problematic in the steep-sided valleys of Scotland. Even where this was achieved, such as at Drumlanrig Castle, Dumfries and Galloway, the ruggedness of the site still achieves a more dramatic tone than formal designs in lowland areas (Wilson 1991, 26–7). Today it is difficult to imagine that the rocky burn in the valley below these gardens is that shown on a plan by John Rocque of c 1739 to have been turned into a formal canal, with a spectacular cascade on its far bank facing the castle (Inigo Triggs 1989, 48). Late 19th-century OS plans still show the elaborate *parterres*. Despite periods of neglect and later alterations, Drumlanrig remains one of the finest examples of a formal garden in northern Europe.

The consequence of the different type of landscape in much of Scotland was that garden designs frequently tended to be squeezed into areas that did not always allow for true symmetry. It is possible that this factor led to Scottish designs forming their own peculiarities. Even when sites were relatively flat, as at Caroline Park, near Edinburgh, the formality of the late 17th- and early 18th-century gardens there contains elements of asymmetry. Although the small burn on the west side of this site contributes towards the lack of true symmetry, the ground is reasonably flat on the east and yet the early 18th-century design remains esoteric. Much of the gardens disappeared under industrial activity during the later 19th century and a recent evaluation on the site of the gardens found survival highly variable. The only archaeology encountered was the foundations of former garden walls and areas of gravel-surfaced roads approaching the house (Ponsford 2003, 325–6).

Archaeology has been used extensively at Chatelherault, Hamilton, an elaborate hunting lodge built between 1732 and 1743 to a design by William Adam for the Duke of Hamilton. Excavation of the *parterre* to the rear of the Banqueting Hall in the 1980s revealed the partial remains of the design, which showed up as areas of contrasting light and dark soils. No gravel or edging to the beds was discovered, but the remains were sufficient to enable the missing portions to be guessed (see Cruft 1991, 179–81, figs 14.9 & 14.10). Further work was undertaken in the mid-1990s on the Bowling Green, a raised earthwork beyond the *parterre* area. This showed that there had been a formal design here overlying the dump of crushed stone and redeposited earth that made up the earthwork. This was designed to be viewed from an adjoining mount (Ponsford & Jackson 1996, 293; 1997, 303).

Figure 48: RAF vertical photograph of Caroline Park dated 23rd June 1961, showing one of Scotland's finest post-medieval mansions with its former designed landscape swamped by industrial development. Copyright RCHMS (53/RAF/4488).

More recently work has been undertaken on the ruins of Cadzow Castle, which is part of the former estates of the Dukes of Hamilton, adjoining Chatelherault. This ruin dates from the medieval period, having been extensively rebuilt in the 16th century. Excavations there in 2002 showed that the ruins had been much altered in the 19th century, probably between 1813 and 1820 by the tenth Duke of Hamilton as part of a deliberate romanticism of the site (Ponsford 2002, 364–5), thus demonstrating that the designed landscaping undertaken on the Hamilton estates was not confined to areas around the main buildings.

Work on the site of the new Scottish Parliament building in Edinburgh revealed evidence for the formal gardens of Queensbury House that included plant beds and tree pits (Ponsford 2001, 204). More recent evaluation at Stevenson House, East Lothian, also produced hopeful signs. Here the apparent remains of an unknown formal garden were discovered – reported as having the potential to provide relatively undisturbed archaeology (Ponsford 2003, 319).

Recent work at Valleyfield House, the only Scottish garden to be designed by the 'English Landscape Garden' designer, Humphrey Repton, in 1801, has recovered a number of structures associated with Repton layout (Ponsford 2000, 348–9). The design was made slightly before 1800 for Sir Robert Preston, and was frequently visited by travellers heading north. There included the radical writer, William Cobbett, who was much impressed by features such as the walled flower garden, the

125

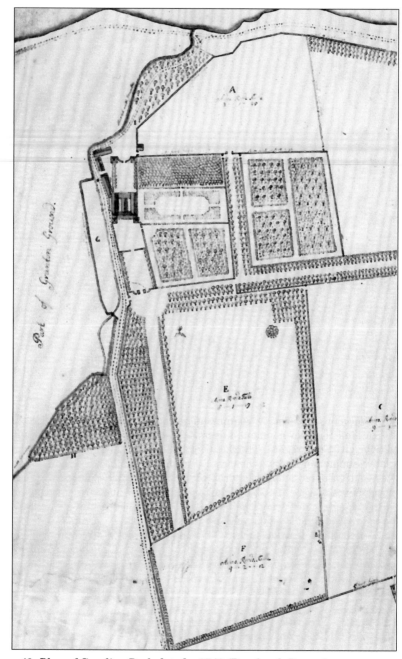

Figure 49: Plan of Caroline Park dated c 1740 (Buccleuch Papers).

ornamental pond, and the rustic bridges over the Bluther Burn. The commencement of this work is particularly encouraging as Valleyfield was a site picked out by Cruft in her 1991 summary of the state of Scottish garden archaeology as being 'a magnificent subject for the application of garden archaeology' (Cruft 1991, 184).

One of the most interesting pieces of work in recent years has been the archaeological recording that has been undertaken as part of the reinstatement of the largely 18th-century water gardens in the grounds of Newhailes, East Lothian – described in detail in the case study within this chapter.

Our knowledge of Scottish gardens has recently been updated by two useful publications. Mackay (2001) gives a good general overview of many of the major gardens from an historian's viewpoint, whilst Robertson (2000) concentrates on the period between 1650 and 1750, referencing some of the sites explored by archaeology.

Some gardens and designed landscapes in Scotland have a form of non-statutory protection if they are one of the 275 places included in the 1987 *Inventory of Gardens and Designed Landscapes*. The *Inventory* was begun in 1982 as a joint project between the predecessors of Scottish Natural Heritage (SNH) and Historic Scotland, leading to the publication of five volumes for the whole of Scotland. However, it was soon recognised that the published sites did not in fact represent all the important gardens in the country, and the *Inventory* is in the process of being supplemented by a further series of volumes. That for Lothians was published in 1997, and Highlands and Islands in 2003, adding a further 53 sites to the total. For the first time, the supplementary volumes specifically recognise the importance of archaeology in gardens and designed landscapes. Work continues on supplements for the rest of Scotland, although progress is slow – leading to some local authorities, including Fife and East Dunbartonshire, undertaking their own surveys of designed landscapes and historic gardens.

If a garden or designed landscape is included on the original 1987 *Inventory*, then it gains some protection. The Town and Country Planning (General Development Procedure)(Scotland) Order 1992 requires planning authorities to consult SNH and Historic Scotland if a development affects an *Inventory* site, and their advice is expected to be given due regard. The fact that this legislation does not cover the sites on the later supplements, or other as yet unlisted important historic designed landscapes and gardens, may be addressed in forthcoming changes to Scotland's planning system.

Historic Scotland and SNH have promised to publish the Inventories on-line in due course. Meanwhile, the boundaries and further details of *Inventory* sites and archaeological intervention on them are available on-line through the RCAHMS Pastmap and Canmore web-based resources.

(See end of Section for notes)

SCOTTISH GARDEN ARCHAEOLOGY: A CASE STUDY

By Robin Turner

Since the early 1990s there has been a steady increase in garden archaeology in Scotland. The National Trust for Scotland has been an active champion of this, recognising the immense benefits of using archaeological techniques as part of the process of revealing the secrets of these fascinating places.

Perhaps the most intensive archaeological study of a Scottish garden has been at Newhailes, a late 17th-century villa on the eastern fringe of Edinburgh. For almost two years, in 2002–3, Abigail Daly was the first archaeologist in Scotland to be employed solely to investigate and interpret a designed landscape: her work, and that of other archaeologists, historians and volunteers, has transformed our understanding of the landscape and how it was used.

Newhailes House was built by the influential architect James Smith in 1686, and was substantially enlarged in the 1720s and 30s by the Dalrymple family. At this time, the framework was put in place to create a modest pleasure ground; this evolved over the next hundred years, but has remained relatively untouched in more recent times. In the 18th century Newhailes housed one of the largest private libraries in the country, and the well-educated owners were significant figures in Edinburgh society during the Scottish Enlightenment. The landscape around the house therefore reflected this scholarship and culture.

Extensive desk-based research was carried out during the conservation of the property, as it was being prepared for opening to the public. This went hand-in-hand with an intensive programme of historic building recording, archaeological survey and investigation. A wealth of old maps and historical documents were found to exist, proving invaluable in understanding and interpreting the physical remains in the landscape.

An archaeological field survey recorded the most obvious landscape features, including: the shell house or grotto; a tea house for taking tea; an ice house and associated curling pond; an interesting doocot; and a raised walk (Ladies Walk) across the pasture fields. Other built features were also noted: walls (some heated), fences, paths, glass houses, an early mushroom house, and the features of a relict water garden. 'Soft' features of the landscape were also recorded, such as planting beds, glades, areas of woodland, and individual trees over 100 years old.

Investing in all this documentary and field research paid dividends in taking forward our understanding of the landscape, and led us to look more closely at some of the features, particularly the water gardens. These were created purely for the enjoyment of visitors to the house, and we were amazed at the extent to which the landscape had been changed and manipulated. The burn that formed the basis of the feature had been canalised in some places, culverted in others, and made into cascades and waterfalls. Bridges crossed the water, and there were several elaborate pools. All this was confirmed through numerous keyhole excavations – a technique causing minimal disturbance, which was also used to trace the routes of historic paths so that they might be re-used in the future.

Our work showed that the water gardens were a place where one could stroll, listening to the varying sounds of the water features, admiring the plants and foliage,

Figure 50: Shell house at Newhailes (© Robin Turner, National Trust for Scotland)

and taking in the scent as it changed from place to place. All the senses were stimulated. But the most spectacular feature was the shell house.

At first sight the shell house is a rather ugly creation: grotto-like at the front, and ruined inside since the middle of the last century. However, correspondence of the 1790s tells how shells were collected from far-flung places to adorn the walls in exotic and intricate patterns. Close examination of the 'grotesque' frontage showed that it had been made with the greatest of care, encrusted with specially modified industrial waste to create a rustic yet interesting effect. As well as shells, the interior had been decorated with broken 18th-century glass and pottery, mirrors and even lapidary offcuts, to create a 'cave of jewels'.

Archaeological examination of the shell grotto showed that special flues had been built into the walls: not for heating, but for creating a smoky aura around the building. In front of the entrance we discovered an intricate cascade, where water would have danced its way into an ornamental pool.

We can now begin to imagine the scene that visitors might have encountered. Standing across the pool, the building would have glinted in the eerie artificial mist, its reflection distorted in the ripples of the cascade. On entering the building, the splendour of ten thousand shells – both local and from other side of the world – would have amazed those educated enough to appreciate them.

Much of this information would have remained hidden had it not been for the concerted programme of archaeological and documentary research. The significance of many things we discovered might also have been unrecognised had we not been able to call on many different specialists to help us interpret them: from garden historians to experts on historic trees. Yet most of this work has been non-invasive, and even the excavations have been small-scale yet very informative.

The Trust's work at Newhailes, and at many other places in Scotland, clearly demonstrates the value of an archaeological approach to historic gardens and landscapes: more and more such investigations are now being carried out in Scotland, often by or with the help of amateur groups.

Chapter 16: Garden archaeology in Wales

By Martin Locock

Garden archaeology in Wales has developed alongside its practice in England, although the regulatory framework is different and the number of projects is much smaller. The Welsh Historic Gardens Trust was founded in 1989, aiming to raise the profile of garden sites and to campaign for their protection. At the same time, Cadw: Welsh Historic Monuments started work on a register of important gardens. An overview of Welsh gardens was published in 1992 (Whittle 1992). The Historic Gardens register was compiled on a county by county basis (using the 1974–1996 counties); the first (Gwent) was completed in 1994, and the final volumes appeared in 2002. Although not a statutory designation, the gardens in the register are graded in line with Listed Buildings (Grades I, II* and II). Registered parks and gardens are usually covered by specific policies in Unitary Development Plans, and since the issuing of *Planning Guidance Wales* in 2002 they have been identified as a material interest in planning terms (para 6.5.23). When developments are proposed affecting gardens on the Register, it is often found that the garden boundaries as defined on the citation, and their associated 'essential setting' and key views, are very closely drawn around the property, and Cadw and others have objected to proposals lying outside these limits because of the effect on the setting or on garden features outside the published boundary.

Perhaps the most distinctive feature of the protection of parks and gardens in Wales is its integration with other forms of spatial planning. The Register's scope was extended to cover other historic landscapes (as Part 2 of the Register, prepared by Cadw, the Countryside Council for Wales (CCW), ICOMOS UK and the Welsh Archaeological Trusts, subsequently published in two pan-Wales volumes, *Register of Landscapes of Outstanding Historic Interest in Wales,* 1998 and *Register of Landscapes of Outstanding Historic Interest in Wales,* 2001). Historic gardens have also been identified as key interests in the CCW's *LANDMAP* multi-disciplinary landscape characterisation studies, which have been completed for all of Wales. In the future, the management of historic parks and gardens may move beyond the traditional inward-looking site focus by exploiting these tools.

Excavations on garden sites have been relatively rare in Wales. The Royal Commission on Ancient and Historical Monuments in Wales (RCAHMW) has undertaken aerial, ground and building survey on specific sites (Briggs 1991; 1997; 1998), and has also added basic records of gardens shown on the 1880s Ordnance Survey mapping to the National Monuments Record. It remains the case, however, that information about those gardens not included on the Register is very limited. The Welsh Historic Gardens Trust is preparing a project to build up a gazetteer of all gardens, although progress to date has been patchy, relying on the enthusiasm of regional branches (notably Carmarthenshire and the Vale of Glamorgan). The details of individual gardens, Registered or not, have been clarified by analysis and research (eg Whittle's continuing investigation of Raglan Castle), often without resort to excavation, through desk-top study, checking of aerial photographs, map research and structural recording.

Conventional excavation of the Lodge Hill Roman cremation cemetery in Caerleon revealed a designed garden landscape setting for the burials; the garden layout has since been discussed at more length (Locock and Howell in press). A supposed motte in the garden of the Rectory at Panteg, Torfaen, was excavated in 1989 and shown to be a natural feature, crowned by a 19th-century summer house (Locock 1998). Excavations in a car park on part of Chippenham Park, Monmouth, revealed a path and planting holes dating from the laying out of the Park as a formal public space in the early 1900s. The National Trust has undertaken excavations in the gardens at Llanerchaeron, Ceredigion, although the main interest of the site was the evidence for a preceding medieval settlement. Some garden evidence was recovered from Cadw's lengthy programmes of consolidation works at Laugharne Castle, Carmarthenshire, and Haverfordwest Priory, Pembrokeshire. Fishpond Wood cascade at The Gnoll, Neath, is discussed elsewhere in this volume.

At Middleton Hall (the National Botanical Garden for Wales), Carmarthenshire, William Paxton had created a landscape park as the setting for a new house in the late 18th century (Briggs 1991). The house and many garden features had been demolished by the 1930s. Dyfed County Council handed the garden to an independent trust in 1995 to develop it as a National Botanic Garden for Wales. The garden opened in 2000 but was soon in severe financial straits due to lower than forecast visitor figures. As part of the recent re-branding as Middleton, there is much more emphasis on the surviving historical features, and a programme of archaeology and restoration has been carried out on the large double-walled garden. The archaeological results were limited, but identified the framework of paths, which now form the basis of a replanted garden.

John Dillwyn Llewellyn, owner of Penllergare, north-west of Swansea, Glamorgan from 1831, transformed it into an extensive woodland park, with a walled garden and Orchid House, and two large lakes with dams and cascades. Housing and other developments in the area since the late 1980s have triggered a variety of archaeological recording works. RCAHMW undertook a survey of buildings around the walled garden; in response to issues raised through the planning process, Bellway Homes commissioned Glamorgan Gwent Archaeological Trust to undertake a survey of the original Lower Lake water-control structures and a watching brief elsewhere. The Penllergare Trust commissioned Cambria Archaeology to survey the important orchid house and the walled garden; and also to compile an integrated GIS database of the park, combining map data, archaeological and historical features, and ecological and landscape data in a series of layers, allowing ready identification of potential management issues.

In 1998, the IFA Wales/Cymru group hosted a well-attended day-school on Garden Archaeology in Wales; a volume of proceedings is in the late stages of preparation, which should demonstrate the wide range of gardens types and approaches to them that have been adopted in the course of this work throughout Wales (Briggs in press).

Figure 51: Looking across the restored Orangery Garden at Tredegar with the mansion in the background. Both Locock and Currie worked on this site as environmental advisers to the excavator and can confirm the excavated evidence for colour bands of earth. It is said that garden historians were dissatisfied with the garden because of its lack of horticultural interest, but gardens of the early 18th century often have spartan designs. (Photo by Martin Locock)

TREDEGAR HOUSE: A MINERAL GARDEN

Tredegar House is large mansion and park on the south-east outskirts of Newport, in the old county of Monmouthshire. The mansion was built by Sir Charles Morgan from 1675 onwards as the focus of a landscaped park and set of formal walled gardens. In the 1680s, an extensive stable block was built to the west of the house, surrounded by walled enclosures, one of which, in 1791, became the Orangery garden. De Bois Landscape Survey Group undertook a programme of geophysical survey, evaluation and excavation of the garden in the late 1980s and early 1990s prior to restoration (Ewart & Phibbs unpublished). The excavations demonstrated the survival of a complex *parterre* garden from the initial Orangery phase, bedded on clay covering an earlier garden. This surface was covered by gravel paths, areas of clay (in contrasting colours), and panels bounded by borders of coal dust, lime and coarsely-crushed shell. There were, in addition, planting holes for individual shrubs and trees, and larger beds. By the late 1700s, this garden had in turn been covered by further dumping.

The results of the excavation work were unexpected in the context of the geophysical survey (which had identified features lying closer to the 1989 ground surface), and the implications provoked doubts among some garden historians, since it was felt that the coloured surfaces would have been impractical under wear and weathering, and that the minimal amount of vegetation was improbable. Whittle, writing shortly after the excavation, concluded that 'the multi-coloured effect of this garden is now hard to imagine' (1992, 32).

Fortunately, Newport Borough Council proceeded to recreate the garden in the mid 1990s, and it is therefore possible to appreciate it as more than a paper reconstruction. The maintenance of the *parterres* requires regular work, and visitors are asked to walk only on the gravel paths. Nevertheless, the garden design is a pleasant complement to the Orangery and the other buildings, and, set off by the carefully trimmed trees, present an opportunity to appreciate the attractions of a formal, geometric, architectural style of garden design which is alien to modern tastes.

ABERGLASNEY: A CONTROVERSIAL GARDEN

It is unfortunately commonplace for the interpretation of gardens to be controversial, but even within the garden world, Aberglasney stands out as exceptional, ever since a presentation by the inaugural meeting of the Welsh Historic Gardens Trust by Prof Dixon Hunt in 1990 (Samuels & Dixon Hunt 1991). The debate has continued ever since, reflected in a lengthy account by Briggs (1999) and Blockley and Halfpenny's excavation report (2002), alongside the restoration and re-opening of the garden.

Aberglasney is situated on the north side of the Tywi valley between Llandeilo and Carmarthen in Carmarthenshire, near the hillfort of Grongar Hill. The site was entered from the north-west through a gatehouse; the large multi-phase house (with elements dating to the early 17th century) is now largely ruinous. To the southwest of the house, the land drops sharply, and the area immediately adjacent to the house is now occupied by an enclosed 'Cloister Garden' with internal arches and a terrace walk above. Other gardens lay to the north, south and west, including a yew tunnel running from the house to the gatehouse. The key associations of the House are with Bishop Rudd (Bishop of St David's, 1594–1614) and his descendants, and with John Dyer, author of the landscape poems 'Grongar Hill' and 'Country Walk' in 1726. Whether any garden features can be linked to these individuals is the main area of contention.

The Gardens Trust's visit in 1990 took place at a time when the site was close to total loss. The house was becoming unsafe and had been partly damaged and robbed; the other structures were overgrown and nearing collapse, while the garden was overgrown. In 1994, the Aberglasney Restoration Trust was founded, and after buying the house and gardens in 1995 it sought numerous grants. In 1998, the restoration project began, and by 2000 it was open to the public. Archaeological work has a longer history, starting with a small excavation in and around the Gatehouse in 1961–62 (Briggs 1999), geophysical survey of the Cloister Garden in 1991 (see Geophysical Survey); structural survey and trial excavations by Lesley Howes Archaeological Services, 1992, evaluation by Dyfed Archaeological Trust, 1995, survey and dendrochronology by RCAHMW and others; and excavation and watching brief by Cambrian Archaeological Projects, 1998–2000 (Blockley & Halfpenny 2002). It is worth noting in passing that the most important single feature, the early cobbled surface at the top of the Cloister Garden, was not located by any of the three sets of evaluation trenching in the area, nor by the geophysical survey.

Figure 52: Looking across the restored Cloister Garden at Aberglasney, the site of some of the fiercest garden history controversies of recent years. Is this a 17th-century garden or a piece of 19th-century myth-making? The jury is still out on which faction is correct. (Photo by Martin Locock)

Much of the earlier writing on Aberglasney (which extends back to the early 1800s) has been based on an easy association between the gatehouse, house, yew tunnel and 'cloister' as representing a late medieval or early post-medieval survival. This is unfortunate since it has confused the picture enormously; the only 16th century evidence is for the presumed predecessor to the early 17th-century house. The attractive equation of Aberglasney with the fine house and nine gardens described by a late medieval poet advanced by Williams (1961) and Jones: 'Rhydderch ap Rhys lived in his house at Llangathem, praised by Lewis Glyn Cothi; of dressed stone, whitewashed, environed by gardens, orchards and vineyards...' (Jones 2002, 219). This association has now been reluctantly abandoned.

The Yew Tunnel was argued to be 'a thousand years old' right up to its removal as part of the restoration project, in the course of which ring counting of a partial core dated its planting to about 245 years ago (ie 1743); Briggs (1999) has suggested an actual planting date in the early 1800s, while the excavators argue for 1710, based on its likely rate of growth (Blockley & Halfpenny 2002, 65). David (1999) questions whether ring-counting on complex yews is in any case effective. It seems to be very difficult to judge past growth rates, especially with trees close to walls and those with multiple stems.

The Cloister Garden is the earliest and most important feature on the site. As noted, although it has been called the Cloister Garden, it is not medieval, nor monastic, nor a conventional cloister; rather it is a walled garden adjoining the house, with building range at the far (south) side, later complemented by ranges on the other sides, creating a roof-top level walkway reached by stairways on the eastern ends of the additions. The excavated remains have been interpreted as a 17th-century garden with an ornate patterned-cobble area close to the house and parallel narrow linear beds, presumably for planting, covering the remainder of the cloister interior (Period 2); the cobbled area was lifted in the 18th century (Period 3). The deliberate creation of such a 'monastic' garden *de novo* in the post-medieval period is highly unusual, and on the face of it perhaps improbable. Briggs (1999, 258), in his lengthy review of historical and structural evidence has argued that the building ranges are much later, from *c* 1770–1830, and the garden features either misinterpreted or mis-dated (1999, 256–7).

It is perhaps surprising that the detailed evidence remains open to interpretation, since there have been two monographs published about the site, archaeological (Blockley & Halfpenny 2002) and garden historical account (David 1999), in addition to numerous review articles and historical studies. It is a pity that Blockley and Halfpenny devote eleven pages to reprinting in its entirety the Miles and Bridge dendrochronology report from Briggs (1999), at the expense of more precise tabulation of the dating evidence from the excavated contexts. As it is, the pottery evidence as presented by Courtney (2002) poses serious questions about phasing, dating and contamination. His Table 2 shows that of the 168 sherds from Period 2 (ie the 17th century, first garden layout), 47 (27.9%) are what he classifies as 18th–20th century wares, and 9 (5.4%) are 19th–20th-century. The much larger Period 3 assemblage (428 sherds) is dominated by North Devon coarsewares of 17th–18th-century date, but also includes 18 sherds (4.2%) of developed white ware of 19th–20th-century date. Given the difficulties of establishing the site stratigraphy, with extensive disturbance by later features, this equivocal evidence is unhelpful.

But more fundamentally at issue is the date and sequence of the building ranges forming the cloister. The key evidence is that of the survey elevations prepared by Lesley Howes in 1992, prior to any consolidation work, including stone-by-stone drawings of the internal elevations (Blockley & Halfpenny 2002, 3). No structural analysis based on this data has been published; Blockley & Halfpenny publish a re-drawn phased plan and elevation, while Briggs (1999) reproduces an original. In the absence of stone and mortar identifications, it is impossible to make a satisfactorily link between building campaigns and archaeological features.

Thus, despite extensive archaeological investigations, carried out over several years, the dating of the main features remains uncertain, and the attempts to link them to the particular tastes and aspirations of Bishop Rudd, John Dyer, or others are therefore premature.

(See end of Section for notes)

Chapter 17: unusual gardens

INTRODUCTION

This chapter looks at case studies where archaeology has been used on sites that do not quite fit into the neat divisions of 'formal' and 'informal'. They demonstrate that, no matter how much we like to classify things into neat types, there will always be examples that fail to fit. This is all the more likely to occur in garden design, because, like all art, it is so often the subject of an individual's whim. Whereas the majority of people creating large-scale gardens in the past have been prone to follow a fashion, human nature is always such that it will produce the non-conformists and mavericks who wish to be different.

The unusual gardens chosen here as case studies are all unique in their way. These include Shilston Barton, Modbury, Devon, where archaeological recording was undertaken on what may be the only remains of any substance of a 'water theatre'. This form of garden ornamentation was highly popular in Italy and much recommended to English gardeners by Stephen Switzer in the early 18th century, but they do not appear to have been taken up on any scale in these islands.[9]

The second site is Dartington Hall, again in Devon. This site has long defied clear classification. For many years it was thought to be a medieval tiltyard, but there were

Figure 53: Shilston Barton, Devon: the grotto overlooking a pond, with the house on the terrace behind. The steep nature of Devon's valleys suits designs that include striking series of terraces.

Figure 54: Shilston Barton, Devon: The central compartment of the grotto, incorporating the earlier water theatre as its back wall.

serious doubts expressed for this interpretation (Platt 1962), and the idea emerged that the garden was a type of late 17th-century formal garden. Finally, recent research has identified it as an unusual example of what the author calls an 'antiquarian garden'. Dartington is now recognised as being one of the oldest known examples of a garden design deliberately incorporating ruined architectural features as a major part of the design. It would seem that this garden had incorporated ruined arches that had formerly been part of an early Tudor long gallery into the garden design before 1682. The 'antiquarian' feel of the garden was later elaborated on as part of Augustus Pugin's uncompleted plans to turn Dartington into one of the country's most notable examples of the Gothic Revival style.

The third 'unusual' site is the garden of the famous naturalist, the Reverend Gilbert White (1720–93) at Selborne (Hants). White only became well-known after his death. During his lifetime he never rose higher than country curate, and so his garden cannot even be considered that of the country gentry. Here, therefore, we have the garden of a poor cleric that has subsequently only become important because of his writings, most of which were published after his death. White's *Journals*, running to three large volumes, are amongst the most detailed contemporary records we have for a garden of this relatively lowly status. His *Natural History of Selborne* is the fourth most published book in the English language, and this has promoted him to a form of cult status. Early in the 1990s funds were raised to try to restore his garden as a setting for The Wakes Museum, located in his former home. Considerable archaeological work has been undertaken at this site since 1992. White's poverty has meant that many of the 'features' within his garden were highly ephemeral, and the evidence is often very scanty.

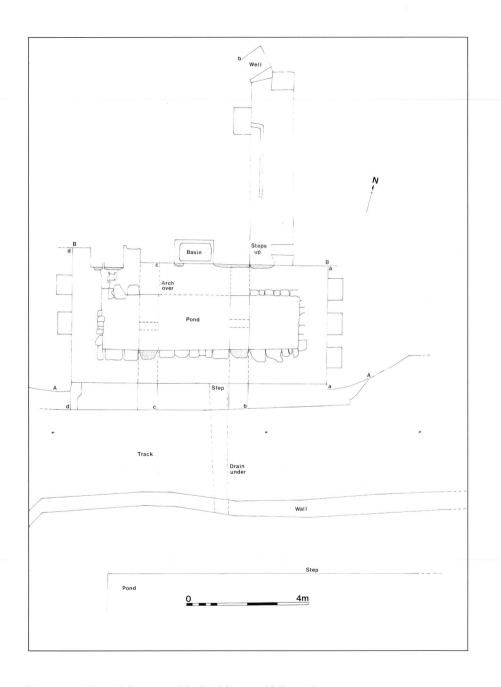

Figure 55: Plan of the grotto-like building at Shilston Barton

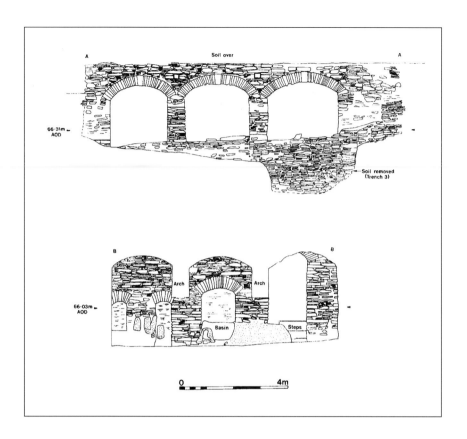

*Figure 56: Front and rear elevations of the grotto-like building at Shilston Barton.
A–A front elevation (south facing). B–B Rear elevation (south facing). See plan (Fig
55) for location of elevations.*

The final site is the pauper's garden belonging to the Southwell Workhouse (Notts),
a site recently taken over by the National Trust. This made a welcome contrast to the
work done of largely aristocratic sites, and showed that even low-status sites can leave
evidence for past activity.

I) SHILSTON BARTON

It could be argued that Shilston fell into the esoteric type of Devonian 17th- and
18th-century garden that existed before the English Landscape garden became the
norm. Although these had formal elements, such as terraces and geometric ponds,
they lacked the overall symmetry of those formal gardens in southern and central
England. It was clearly the more rugged topography of Devon, with its steep narrow
valleys and rocky outcrops, which prevent such symmetry being implemented. Thus
the formal features of many Devon gardens are fitted into the landscape where

140

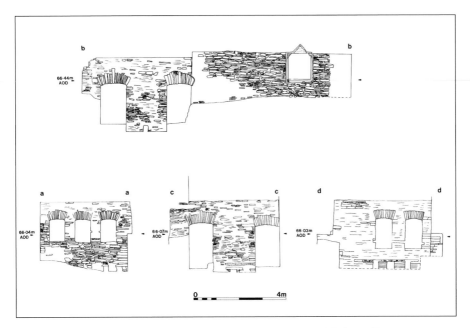

Figure 57: Internal elevations of the grotto-like building at Shilston Barton. a–a internal east wall (west facing). b–b internal wall to spring head (east facing). c–c internal wall, east facing. d–d internal west wall (east facing). See plan (Fig 55) for location of elevations.

circumstances allowed. Not only is this a characteristic of Devon, but many of the gardens in Cornwall, Wales, the Pennines, Scotland, and other more upland regions follow this pattern. Whereas in lowland England warm brick pervaded within formal gardens, in these other regions garden features appear harsher in their native stone. These materials, along with the uneven topography, leave an impression of irregularity in spite of the attempts of the owners to adhere to the formal fashion.

Shilston Barton is no exception. It displays terraces, geometric ponds, a walled garden and a modest cascade (Waterhouse 2003), but it fails to 'feel' formal in a setting that lovers of the late 18th-century Picturesque would have appreciated. But if Shilston is fairly typical of its kind, the garden feature uncovered by its owner during earthmoving operations is not only unusual, but possibly unique in the UK. This feature had the initial appearance of a triple arched grotto overlooking a small rectangular pond set into a hillside. The impression was that it had similarities with William Kent's vanished grotto at Claremont, Surrey, or in the triple arched feature in the Vale of Venus at Rousham (Oxon), another of Kent's designs.

However, careful examination of the structure showed that the triple arch front had been added to the back wall of an earlier 'grotto'. The original feature was a narrow tunnel cut into the rocky hillside leading to a stone well. On either side was a rustic stone wall almost three metres high revetting a large terrace in front of the house. Set into this wall are a series of alcoves, a basin, and a number of outlets from which water, collected from springs in the hillside, could be made to pour. In front of this was a rectangular pond 6.4m by 1.8m, with a stepped channel leading from it into the larger rectangular pond beyond. In its heyday the play of water from the outlets in the wall would have been most entertaining. One of the exits for water appears to be between the legs of a carved figure, possible a Pan or a Sheila-na-gig, but such is the erosion to the structure it is no longer possible to tell what it was originally.

Such plays of water were well known in Italian Renaissance gardens. Stephen Switzer shows many illustrations of them in his 1729 book, *A universal system of water and water-works, philosophical and practical*, a treatise on ornamental water features for gardens. They were commonly known as 'water theatres' by contemporaries. There are no known extant examples of such 'theatres' in the UK (Currie 2003, 60–65), although it is possibly just a matter of recognising their remains.

In essence, the work at Shilston was more in keeping with building recording than excavation. Despite digging trenches in front of the structure, and on top, the interpretation of the site came mainly from the structural recording, and how it fitted in with the overall history of the site and tentative parallels elsewhere. As has been shown through the author's work on cascades (*cf* Currie *et al* 1994), features that were once considered rare in the UK have since become relatively commonplace following their initial recognition and publication. It is hoped that the publication of the Shilston water theatre (Currie 2003) will prompt further discoveries of such features elsewhere.

II) DARTINGTON HALL

Work at Dartington Hall started out with a very simple premise suggested by the gardens manager, Graham Gammin. This was to disprove the local tradition that a three-sided terraced feature in a steep coomb was a medieval tiltyard.[10] This was achieved within the first proper season of digging, not through excavation, but from the accidental discovery of a photograph of the area as a formal garden in the 1860s. As excavation work progressed further, the results were largely disappointing, and once

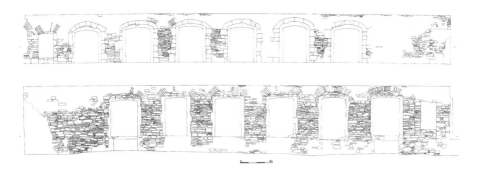

Figure 58: Surveyor's drawing of the ruined arcade at Dartington, part of a late medieval and Tudor South Court demolished in the years just before 1682 and incorporated into the design of the Best Garden. This possibly makes it the earliest example of including 'antiquarian' ruins into the design of a post-medieval garden . Top, north facing elevation. Bottom, south facing elevation.

again it was the examination and recording of standing structures and an examination of historical sources that eventually solved the riddle of the Dartington garden.

The initial impression was that the terraces at Dartington Hall were part of a late 17th- or early 18th-century formal garden. This was seemingly supported by the presence of a line of very old sweet chestnut trees on the top of the upper terrace on the far side of the coombe. These eventually proved to be a red herring.

It seemed that the most obvious way to approach the problem posed at Dartington was to prove that the terraces were once part of a garden. So, before the photographic proof was found later in the week, trenches were laid out on the terraces to try to recover evidence of garden activity. Nothing was forthcoming. Elsewhere a trench was dug to examine a parch mark at the far end of the 'Bowling Green' (one of the upper terraces on the hall side of the coombe), and another was excavated on the Best Lawn to try to recover evidence for an apparent garden building shown on the 1839 tithe map). The latter was thought to be on or near the site of a building called the 'tower', a structure partly excavated by Colin Platt in 1962 as part of the lost south courtyard at Dartington (Platt 1962). It was originally thought that this building had been retained as a garden structure, but this did not prove to be the case. The structure shown in 1839 must have been an ephemeral building with a very short life span. It was not, in retrospect the tower, nor was it shown on a painting and plans dating from the early 19th century. Whatever it was may never be known as the unfolding results led to much change in the original project design.

Although work continued on the area around the tower for the full eight seasons, this work eventually proved largely irrelevant to an understanding of the garden. Excavation here did determine that the south courtyard of the hall had been demolished in the later 17th or early 18th century, information that had already been determined in Colin Platt's earlier excavation. The exact date that the courtyard was demolished, and the Best Garden terrace laid out on its site, was eventually determined by documentary research. A deed dated 1682 records 'the Newhouse on the north side of the garden called the fine garden' (Currie 2003, 54–55), a clear indication that the post-medieval wing on the west side of the hall was already in existence at this time, and that the courtyard had been replaced by the Best Garden.

Excavation of a garden wall at the east end of the Bowling Green dated this also to the end of the 17th century, identifying it as an extension of a series of walls built to surround the Best Garden. This wall was found to include the ruined arches of a structure thought to be a Late medieval/Tudor long gallery (Platt 1962). These arches had been crucial to the earlier discussion as to whether the terraces below formed an amphitheatre around a 14th-century tiltyard, as it was argued that they formed a viewing position for the jousting (Hussey 1938, 208).[11] Subsequent research found that the Tiltyard myth had been invented by the Elmhirsts after they purchased the property in 1926. They even altered the terraces to an imagined 14th-century form, removing the evidence for the formal garden that had existed there previously.

By the mid-point in the excavations it became clear that the ruined arches were crucial to the understanding of the garden, and it was decided to undertake a measured survey of the structure. This determined that they had probably been erected in the early Tudor period as part of a second courtyard. What was remarkable about these arches was that they had been deliberately incorporated into the walls of a garden that was in existence by 1682. This was a very early date to include an antiquarian 'Gothic' ruin into a garden, particularly an early formal garden. It had previously been thought that the incorporation of antiquarian ruins into garden design was something that occurred largely from the 1740s onwards. What we appeared to have at Dartington was a deliberate attempt to enhance the air of antiquity of the place in the later 17th century. This had been undertaken by the Champernowne family, owners of the hall from the 16th century to the 1920s, as a way of demonstrating their status as one of Devon's oldest landed families.

What was even more remarkable was that this contrived antiquarianism did not end with the incorporation of the ruined arches into a 17th-century formal garden, but it continued into the 19th century. Having failed to find any evidence for the formal garden by excavation, the author was forced to resort to further documentary research. It was this work that finally resolved the problem. A series of drawings and plans in the Devon Record Office revealed that in the first half of the 19th century two successive Champernownes toyed with the idea of recreating a 'Gothick' south courtyard, again to enhance their status as an ancient family. Plans of the first attempt in 1805 survive that show the gardens as they were at that date. Much to everyone's surprise, they did not show an old formal garden on the site of the terraces. Instead they showed an ornamental pond in the valley bottom, which helped explain the undated stone drains that were the sole archaeological evidence to survive the Elmhirsts' remodelling in the 1920s. In the 1840s another attempt was made to revive the scheme, this time employing Augustus Pugin, one of the great protagonists of the Gothic Revival. Although no plans survive to show the terraced garden at this time (they had been notably absent from the tithe map of 1839), it is probably no coincidence that it first appears in a photograph dated to the late 1860s. Although Pugin's scheme for an elaborate Gothic courtyard were never carried out, it would seem that work began making the terraces as a formal revivalist garden.

In the end it was a combination of methods that solved the riddle of the Dartington garden. Excavation, building recording, topographic analysis and documentary research were all responsible for producing the final picture. Although excavation had hinted at the sequence of events, it had been unable to dissolve fully the mist of antiquarian 'deception' that had hung over the gardens, a process that had been begun by the Champernownes at some time before 1682. This was further compounded by the removal of primary archaeological evidence in the 1920s. Just prior to the discovery of the documentary evidence that clinched the final solution, those involved in the project were broadly aware that a sequence roughly similar to what eventually proved to be the truth must have occurred, but the final proof was even more remarkable than the supposition derived from the fieldwork. In all honesty the author had concluded the original formal garden, with ruined arches, was laid out around 1720–40, and that the terraces beyond could have been either part of that scheme or part of a post-1839 formal revivalist scheme (remembering the terraces were not shown on the tithe map). In the final event the original formal garden turned out to be a remarkable survival of what can best be described as 'antiquarian' design, and, dating from before 1682, it is the earliest example recognised in the UK to date. The cherry on the cake was that the formal revivalist terracing in the valley below the older garden was associated with further antiquarian proposals suggested by Augustus Pugin. The tiltyard myth was eventually laid to rest, but only with the realisation that the myth-making at Dartington could no longer be laid solely at the feet of the Elmhirsts, but with successive generations of owners stretching back three centuries.

III) THE WAKES

David Standing, the head gardener at The Wakes, began his career by obtaining an MA in Environmental Science. This academic background has stood him in good stead as he has since become a tremendously knowledgeable authority on the works of the Reverend Gilbert White, creator of a thoroughly unusual minor cleric's garden at The Wakes in the 18th century. He describes it thus:

> White's garden appears to have consisted of a small holding of some seven acres consisting of orchards, vegetable plots, flower gardens and a miniature landscape garden. This contained Ha-has, urns, alcoves, obelisks, rustic seats, a statue and a mount. Working out the layout of the garden has posed a number of problems as no map or plan of the grounds has been found which shows the details of White's design. The main source of information is his gardening diary, the Garden Kalendar, which he kept between 1751 and 1771, and whilst this contains a number of clues, it is like a huge prose jigsaw, continued (although in less detail) by his natural history journals (1768–1793) (Standing 2004).

Excavations have been undertaken there from time to time since 1992. The work began as a method to answer some of the more important outstanding questions concerned with the restoration of the garden. Since then the author has been called back both to inform proposed new works and to undertake watching briefs.

Figure 59: The Wakes, Selborne (Hants): The garden of the famous naturalist, Gilbert White, looking toward the multi-period house.

Many of White's features were highly ephemeral, such as his 'statue' of Hercules or his Alcove. The former was little more than a painted cardboard cut-out placed to be seen from a distance where it appeared to be a real statue. The Alcove was merely a wooden shelter near the end of a ha-ha. The remains found on the conjectured site of this feature were no more than a single post-hole and a short stone edging (Currie 1995c, 196–7). Initial excavation in the garden seemed to suggest that White's features were made of the scantiest materials until the terminal of one of his paths was located.

These were highly unusual. They were narrow, barely 0.6m wide, and made of uneven lumps of a coarse local stone called ragstone. Clearly designed for the passage of a single person around the garden, these paths were entirely unlike those found in aristocratic gardens, where the main circulatory paths were invariable wide enough to allow at least two people to walk along them conversing. White's singularly narrow paths seem to have been made simply for himself to get around dry shod to carry out maintenance and make observations. As an unmarried cleric it seems he had not conceived of the notion of walking around the garden in anyone's company. Although White had visitors, mainly his relations and academics who shared his naturalist interests, the paths were not designed for leisurely strolling. If anything their uneven nature required them to be traversed with great caution. These paths did not seem to follow any grand design, and were discovered unexpectedly on every occasion they appeared. They existed simply to get White from his house to specific parts of the garden. It is suspected that one such path led to a now vanished barn that stood near the top of Baker's Hill.

It is of some interest that after a second discovery of part of a stone path was made, the gardens were offered the services of a local dowser to determine the route between the two fragments identified to date. The author did not meet this man, but he was clearly of an upstanding appearance as his highly unusual interpretation of the path's course was taken seriously by people who command the highest respect. The dowsed interpretation suggested a path that wound snake-like up the hill in the most unbelievable manner. Although the author expressed his doubts as to the likelihood of these conjectures, he was asked to test the results by excavation. Once this was completed, it seemed doubtful that the dowser had been correct at any stage. The snake-like path simply did not exist, nor did any other feature along its hypothetical line. The true line of the path, as revealed by excavation, followed the shortest possible route between the two previously exposed sections, confirming the author's view that White's curious stone paths were purely utilitarian, as were much of his gardening efforts.

White's journals show that, for the most part, he used his garden to produce fruit and vegetables for his own consumption. On occasion his naturalistic instincts made him adopt experiments to see if he could improve on time-honoured methods of kitchen gardening, but, in the main, he was concerned with practical matters. There were elements of ornament within the wider garden, such as his cardboard Hercules and flimsy Alcove, but these were little more than items of whimsy.

Recovering archaeology at such a garden was not easy, but it was important to make the effort. White's garden was typical of the type of garden that Turner (1992) considers should merit more of our attention. This writer considers that our interest in aristocratic gardening has been to the detriment of the gardens of the poorer classes. In examining the garden of this relatively poor cleric an attempt has been made to redress the balance.

Nonetheless, White was still a member of the educated classes, and he understood the classical allusions in aristocratic gardens. His 'statue' of Hercules was a poor man's attempt to imitate at least part of the imagery of the cultured classes.

IV) THE WORKHOUSE, SOUTHWELL

It is only by turning to the workhouse at Southwell, Nottinghamshire, that it is possible to truly appreciate the gardening of the poor, even if it was overseen by the middle classes. This huge brick institution was begun in 1824, and encouraged the pauper inmates to undertaken kitchen gardening on plots around the site to produce fruit and vegetables for their consumption.

Work here in 1999 showed, once again, the resilience of planting beds in the archaeological context. The pinkish soils of the Midland counties often act as a startling contrast to the dark organic soils dug into linear planting beds on such sites. Although the lines of the beds at Southwell did not stand out as well as those in the Rose Garden at Castle Bromwich Hall (*cf* Currie & Locock 1991a, Figs 3 & 4), sufficient remained less than 100mm below the surface to make them readily distinguishable. Also visible at Southwell were slightly more substantial linear planting beds alongside the remaining paths. These were interpreted as edging plants, possibly box or something similar. It was then of great interest to discover in the accounts for the workhouse that box was purchased for the purpose of edging (Ponsford 2000, 297). It would appear that even in a pauper's garden such as this, where the main crop was potatoes, that there should be this reference back to the box edging so typical of aristocratic gardens!

To date the grey brown soils in Gilbert White's garden have failed to produce the contrast in colour necessary to distinguish the linear planting beds of kitchen gardening, but the lesson of Southwell shows that even in the most unpromising of gardens of the lowest class in society, archaeological evidence can survive clearly enough to enable useful interpretation of the gardening practices undertaken.

(See end of Section for notes)

Chapter 18: A multi-disciplinary approach to garden archaeology

By Iain Soden

The contents of gardens vary tremendously. They comprise a spectrum of landscape ensembles from apparent wildernesses to the most tightly-managed and manicured compartments. Yet all are transient and in a state of constant change. Even great, visual gardens which seem to embody the greatest landscape architecture change with the seasons and the natural cycle of growth and decay. Such mutability can be seen at Drottningholm, Sweden, often covered in snow for months on end, the ground iron-hard and its fountain-pools frozen.

Archaeology is no guarantor of a beautiful garden reconstruction, since archaeology brings no assurance that our forbears enjoyed the same tastes as our own. Without invasive archaeology an historic-garden reconstruction may be inaccurate, but it need not be ugly. Mature gardens today are one of the best illustrations of changing taste and our ability to appreciate fully what previous generations set out to achieve. Such was the thinking behind the tree-planting of Lancelot Brown, using species which would mature long after his own death. Restoration is perhaps the same long view, just in reverse. Witness the breathtaking vistas of the gardens at Chateau de la Roche Courbon in France, much restored and reconstructed with a degree of originality. They are surely an entirely natural progression of the French style and their pedigree can be traced by the stunned viewer with no particular recourse to archaeology.

Archaeology, however, adds a level of detail that studying changing styles and tastes in hindsight cannot. But it is the very transience of gardens which must be seen as a serious limitation of the evidence. Faced with this transience, garden archaeologists need to understand that no two features which they expose and record, may actually be appearing alongside their original neighbour. Pottery and other finds rarely indicate exact contemporaneity, most types being datable to anything closer than what equates to a generation. Unfortunately few gardens have been examined which enjoy the single-phase layout seen at Hampton Court Palace's Privy Garden. Laid out in 1702, its immediate demise and a gradual return to nature was a major key to the survival of its archaeology. Other such gardens lost to overgrowth, 'fossilised' and then archaeologically investigated include the seminal work at Castle Bromwich Hall (West Midlands; 1986–92) and Kirby Hall (Northamptonshire; 1987–95). A raft of different prospection techniques set the tone for years to come, inevitably with excavation as the test of all that went before. All three of these gardens benefit from good documentary resources, fully researched in concert with the archaeology.

For the more mundane garden, and indeed most gardens with any real longevity, the layouts, the planting schemes, the water table and the personal economic fortunes of their owners make for the constant change which may throw many archaeologists off track if the evidence is pushed too far without corroboration. Gardens may not be gardens for long, and their redevelopment, past or proposed, may endanger all but the most robust elements, such as at the Elizabethan East Garden at Coombe Abbey,

Figure 60: Charterhouse, Coventry 1986. Hand-excavation through 1m of apparently undifferentiated post-medieval garden soils exposed the paths and roof tile-lined planting beds of the medieval monks' cell gardens (Photo by Iain Soden)

Warwickshire. This was barely recognisable without the benefit of contemporary engravings.

If an idea of the original planting is required, then documentary study is absolutely necessary. Many historic gardens enjoyed the benefaction of well-educated owners, patrons, designers, plant-collectors, and in many cases even the gardeners, such as the 18th-century head gardener John Whittingham who diarised his 50 years at the nursery garden at Charterhouse, Coventry (Coventry City Archives 201/1). His diary listed what he planted, where he planted it and added the weather for each day and night for his entire adult life. When his son Charles continued the business for a while after John's death, he published lists of the seeds he produced and sold. Excavations there in 1986–87 revealed planting trenches, garden sheds, planting houses and evidence for animals on site, serving house and garden together. They also found plenty of evidence for simple garden ceramics in the kitchen garden, often matched in numbers by worn out and broken tablewares, probably used for crocking or improving drainage. In a world of strict hierarchies, Whittingham actually enjoyed something of a role-reversal with his eccentric patron, Edward Inge, who built him a folly-cum-store in which to live, then promptly moved in himself, eschewing the comforts of his mansion for months on end. Whittingham himself was perhaps not everyone's idea of a fully rounded character, since amidst his concern for frosts and his beloved Pinks, his wife's death merits only one line, even less than the indignant exclamation of 'The French have taken Guadeloupe; a fleet has been dispatched', one of many contemporary observations. All this was played out over the ruins of Charterhouse, a medieval monastery, now a Scheduled Ancient Monument. Dominated by the monastery's listed buildings, the

Figure 61: Charterhouse, Coventry 1987. Gardens often included animals: this mundane mid-19th-century structure was the base of a copper for boiling up pig-swill, the only evidence that pigs were there at all. (Photo by Iain Soden)

Figure 62: Charterhouse, Coventry. The back of the house across the lawns. The fourteen-acre gardens which were laid out over the monastic remains, were the subject of a detailed gardener's diary from c 1745–90. (Photo by Iain Soden)

buried gardens are an important part of the scheduled landscape, the bones of which have changed comparatively little since 1381, even in the midst of a city. It is the (in this case) daily documentation which is the prime key to understanding more of their history than a mere snapshot afforded by an archaeological trench. It is important to note here that the evidence for garden activity was recorded alongside the remains of the medieval monastery, thus demonstrating how garden archaeology can be integrated into a wider research programme (Soden 1995).

Sourcing the proper plants and matching archaeologically-recovered seeds to reference collections is made easier for everything after the mid-18th century, thanks to the work of one man, Carl Linnaeus (1707–78). His Latin binominal classification is that which is still in use today for all botanical specimens, regularly augmented by new varieties. His own garden also remains in existence, laid out just as his scientific leanings indicated. Each specimen is meticulously labelled.

When planting reconstruction is impossible and the soils of the garden so damaged by recent development or denuded by over-work, only the bare bones may be left. Geophysical prospection and targeted excavation may effectively rediscover the structural compartments and boundaries, such as at the palace of Agreda in Spain. Just as focal architecture formed a nexus in many formal gardens, this has a habit of surviving the ravages of time in a way that the plants and the soils do not. It often also left architect's ideas on paper, invoices, receipts and letters of adoration or complaint. Thus archaeology is often drawn to the architecture such as at Chiswick House, where garden architecture is shown to have failed spectacularly. What has long grown out and lost its intended form, such as planting, can rarely be replaced exactly, but what deteriorates slowly and can be conserved, such as brick or stone, attracts our eye and our attention -and inevitably finances.

Gardens, however, are transient things, taming landscapes for a short time only and we can only understand their intended effects upon the viewer and the visitor if we consider all approaches. These include the intended aspect (view from without), the prospect (view from) and the statements they each made about status, hierarchy, beauty and attitudes to the natural world in each generation or season of their existence. This can only be achieved through rigorous and diligent study of drawn, written and photographic sources as a prelude to the physical search for the archaeological remains. Documents provide context and evidence of intent, trial and error, fancy and the mundane, the vision and the truly experimental. Gardeners were after all (and still are), trying to harness the one thing which will not be harnessed, nature. Archaeology may tell us the result, but it will not tell us the thinking behind the attempt.

SECTION NOTES

1   The methodology is outlined in Locock (1994, 235-41).

2   The water garden at Tackley, Oxon, and moated garden at Lyveden New Bield, Northants are examples of early formal gardens detached from their main houses.

3   The 'field walk' was not my idea, but part of the brief. I seem to remember being opposed to undertaking it.

4   Although a short length of 'cascade' was discovered buried following a change in direction of the stream by the site of a structure known as 'Stamford's Roothouse'. This surprised everyone in being very formal, a linear stone-lined channel with a (possibly later) brick floor.

6   Even in the biased position of being its author, I am able to recognise this point.

7   For details of recent work see 'Post-Medieval Archaeology' (Ponsford, ed) and 'Discovery and Excavation in Scotland' (annual CSA publication, R Turner, ed).

8   For example there are terraced gardens set out on steep hillsides in Devon that have many similarities to Aberdour (cf Waterhouse 2003).

9   James Bond has pointed out that there are very fragmentary remains of water features similar to those found in Italian Renaissance gardens at Hanwell Castle and Enstone in Oxon. The latter is well-known from a contemporary descriptions.

10   The exposure of the tiltyard myth has been published in Currie (2003a, 51–59).

11   Hussey states 'It has been suggested by Mr Elmhirst, in explanation of this remarkable arrangement – and I feel in agreement with him – that the amphitheatre was formed out of a natural dell to provide a tiltyard, and that the arcade [the ruined arches on the south side of the Best Garden] is the remains of a kind of 'grand stand' incorporated in the outer side of the garden court'. This view came to be accepted as an established fact, and has been repeated by Emery (1970) and Snell (1988), despite Platt's (1962) archaeological evidence, later confirmed and strengthened by the author's own work (Currie 2003). Emery (1975) later retracted his earlier view, but continued to maintain a late 14th-century date for the arches, a view not sustained by Platt (*op cit*) or Currie (*op cit*), both considering them to be late 15th- or early 16th-century in date.

SECTION 4: CONCLUSIONS

Chapter 19: Conclusions

It can be seen that garden archaeology was in a relatively primitive state as recently as the 1980s compared with the techniques used on other sites. Plan recovery, a technique long considered to be looking back to 'antiquarian' traditions left behind 50 years ago, was still the principal aim of many relatively recent garden projects. The idea that garden archaeology was capable of far more had not been grasped in the UK. In many ways this has been reflected in our approaches to more general 'historical archaeology'. As closer ties are forged with our North American counterparts, and through the efforts of organisations such as the Society for Post-Medieval Archaeology, the archaeology of the last five hundred years has become more acceptable as an area of serious research.

Another welcome change in recent years is the increasing recognition that 'garden archaeology' is not solely a post-medieval subject. The 1990s saw the publication of a number of articles that began to recognise that medieval gardens have survived as earthworks in the countryside. There has been little excavation work on such sites yet, but the groundwork has been laid for these sites to be investigated in a responsible manner. One of the few medieval sites to reveal garden remains is highlighted by Iain Soden at the Coventry Charterhouse. His call for a more holistic approach to such sites is a timely reminder of the importance of integrating gardens into the wider research framework for sites where they are likely to exist.

Iain also highlights the important point that no matter how good the archaeology might be, it can not fully inform us of the exact thinking behind the garden. For this we are obliged to refer to documents and have knowledge of the social attitudes of the time. Thus, Martin Locock shows us that the restored mineral garden at Tredegar is a reasonably accurate interpretation of the archaeological discoveries, but it was criticised by modern garden enthusiasts for not having enough botanical interest. Tredegar is not the first site where modern taste has failed to understand past attitudes to garden design.

In the archaeology of gardens there is a new world out there waiting to be explored. In doing so we will enrich human knowledge, but, in our efforts to do so, let us hope that we will not get carried away. There have been 'garden archaeology' projects where the enshrined principle of preserving archaeology *in situ* unless there is good reason to do otherwise has not always been followed. Many 'restorations' of historic gardens have ignored the rules that would have been automatically applied to other types of site, and it is not the purpose of this book to fuel further projects of this nature. It is hoped that as garden archaeology slips almost unnoticed into the mainstream of the subject, the rules that apply to archaeology in general will come to be applied to gardens. The next time you hear some one berate garden archaeology as being 'not proper archaeology', remember the same was said of medieval archaeology within living memory. Archaeology is the study of material culture, and that study is valid wherever you seek it. Gardens have much to tell us about human behaviour. We learn much about the meaning of our existence from the study of things, such as gardens, which we often take for granted. At the beginning of creation, our legends tell us the first thing the creator did, having made the world, was not to build a house, or to make weapons or jewellery, it was to make a garden.

FURTHER READING:

Garden history is a popular subject, and it would be an impossible task to list all the publications worthy of reading. It is hoped that the works referenced in the text will be sufficient to guide most people in the subject of garden archaeology. However, there are some other works of reference not used here that might be useful to the reader. The list is short, but then so is space, so, hopefully the following will be sufficient. It is not meant to be comprehensive.

Desmond, R, 1984, *Bibliography of British gardens*, Winchester: St Paul's Bibliographies

Goode, P, & Lancaster, M (eds), 1986, *The Oxford companion to gardens*, Oxford: Oxford University Press

Green, D, 1956, *Gardener to Queen Anne: Henry Wise (1653–1738) and the formal garden*, Oxford: Oxford University Press

A selection of some county and regional surveys of gardens include:

Bond, C J, 1998, *Somerset parks and gardens: a landscape history*, Tiverton: Somerset Books

Cantor, L & Squires, A, 1997, *The historic parks and gardens of Leicestershire and Rutland*, Leicester: Kairos Press

Gray, T, 1995, *The garden history of Devon: an illustrated guide to the sources*, Exeter: University of Exeter Press

Harding, S & Lambert, D, 1994, *Parks and gardens of Avon*, Bristol: Avon Gardens Trust

Lockett, R, 1997, *A survey of historical parks and gardens in Worcestershire*, Worcester: Hereford & Worcester Gardens Trust

Mowl, T, 2002, *Historic gardens of Gloucestershire*, Stroud: Tempus

Pett, D E, 1998, *The parks and gardens of Cornwall*, Penzance: Alison Hodge

Stamper, P, 1996, *Historic parks and gardens of Shropshire*, Shrewsbury: Shropshire County Council

Sheeran, G, 1990, *Landscape gardens in West Yorkshire 1680–1880*, Wakefield: Wakefield Historical Publications

Way, T, 1997, *A study of the impact of imparkment on the social landscape of Cambridgeshire and Huntingdonshire from c 1080 to 1760*, BAR British series no 258, Oxford: British Archaeological Reports

Williamson, T, 2000, *Suffolk's gardens and parks: Designed landscapes from the Tudors to the Victorians*, Macclesfield: Windgather

Back issues of *Garden History* and the *Journal of Garden History* are well worth consulting. They contain many interesting articles space has not allowed me to reference here.

Bibliography

Note: Most unpublished reports cited in this work are referenced according to their entry in the annual round-up articles that appear in the various period journals. For the most part this will be the annual round up in *Post-Medieval Archaeology* (*cf* Ponsford & Jackson 1996).

Adkins, L & Adkins, R A, 1982, *A thesaurus of British archaeology*, London: David & Charles

Alcock, N W, Barley M W, Dixon, P W, & Meeson, R A 1996, *Recording timber-framed buildings: an illustrated glossary*, Practical handbooks in archaeology, no 5, York: CBA, (revised edition)

Alcock, N W, & Hall, L, 1994 *Fixtures and fittings in dated houses 1567–1763*, Practical handbooks in archaeology, no 11, York: CBA

Andrews, D, Blake, B, Clowes, M & Wilson, K, 1995, *The survey and recording of historic buildings*, Technical Paper no 12, Oxford: Association of Archaeological Illustrators & Surveyors

Anthony, J, 1991, *The Renaissance garden in Britain*, Princes Risborough: Shire

Aspinall, A and Pocock, J A 1995, 'Geophysical prospection in garden archaeology: an appraisal and critique based on case studies', *Archaeological Prospection* **2**, 61–84

Aston, M 1978, 'Gardens and earthworks at Hardington and Low Ham, Somerset', *Proc. Somerset Archaeol. 7 Natur. Hist. Soc.*, **122**, 12–17

Aston, M, (ed) 1988, *Medieval fish, fisheries and fishponds in England*, BAR British series no **182**, Oxford: British Archaeological Reports, 2 vols

Atkinson, R J C, 1953, *Field Archaeology*, London: Methuen, (2nd ed; 1st ed 1946)

Bagenal, P, 1994, 'Roxford's forgotten grotto', *Hertfordshire Countryside*, (July 1994), 16–7

Barker, P, 1982, *Techniques of archaeological excavation*, London: Batsford (3rd ed; 1st ed 1977)

Bell, R D, 1990 'The discovery of a buried Georgian garden in Bath', *Garden History*, **18.1**, 1–21

Bell, R D, 1993 'Archaeology and the Rococo Garden: the restoration at Painswick House, Gloucestershire', *Garden History*, **21.1**, 24–45

Beresford, M & St Joseph, J K 1958, *Medieval England: an aerial survey*, Cambridge: Cambridge University Press

Bilikowski, K, 1983, *Historic parks and gardens*, Hampshire's Countryside Heritage no 5, Winchester: Hampshire County Council

Blockley, K and Halfpenny, I, 2002, *Aberglasney House and Gardens: archaeology, history and architecture* (British Archaeological Reports, British Series, 334; Oxford)

Bond, C J, 1978, 'The recording and survey of moats' in Aberg, F A, *Medieval moated sites*, London: CBA Research Report no 17, 14–20

Bond, C J & Tiller, K (eds) 1987, *Blenheim: landscape for a palace*, Stroud: Sutton (2nd ed 1997)

Briggs, C S, 1991, Garden archaeology in Wales, in Brown, A E (ed.) *Garden Archaeology* (CBA Research Report 78, London), 138–159

Briggs, C S, 1997, The fabric of parklands and gardens in the Tywi Valley and beyond, *Carmarthenshire Antiquary* **33**, 88–105

Briggs, C S, 1998, A new field of Welsh cultural history: inference and evidence in gardens and landscapes since *c* 1450, in Pattison, P (ed.) *There by Design: field archaeology on parks and gardens* (RCHME, London), 65–74

Briggs, C S, 1999, Aberglasney: the theory, history and archaeology of a post-medieval landscape, *Post-Medieval Archaeology* **33**, 242–284

Briggs, C S (ed.), In press, *Garden archaeology in Wales*

Britton, F, 1990, 'The Pickleherring Potteries: an inventory', *Post-Medieval Archaeology*, **24**, 61–92

Brown, A E, & Taylor, C C, 1972 'The gardens at Lyveden, Northamptonshire', *Archaeological Journal*, **129**, 154–60

Brown, A E (ed.), 1991 *Garden Archaeology*, London: Council for British Archaeology Research Report **78**

Calkins, R G, 1986, 'Piero de Crescenzi and the medieval garden' in MacDougall, E B, (ed), *Medieval gardens*, Washington: Dumbarton Oaks, 157–73

Campbell, C, 1725, *Vitruvius Brittannicus*, vol. 3, London

Clark, A, 1990, *Seeing Beneath the Soil: Prospecting methods in archaeology*, London: Batsford

Cole, M A, David, A E U, Linford, N T, Linford, P K and Payne, A W, 1997, 'Non-destructive techniques in English gardens: geophysical prospecting', *Journal of Garden History* **17 i**, 26–39

Collier, M, & Wrightson, D, 1993, 'The Recreation of the Turkish Tent at Painshill', *Garden History*, **21.1**, 46–59

Colwell, F, 1986, 'Richard Woods (?1716–93): A preliminary account', *Garden History*, **14.2**, 85–119

Conyers, L, in press, 'Ground penetrating radar exploration and mapping techniques for garden archaeology', in Malek, A (ed.) *Techniques for Garden Archaeology* Washington DC: Dumbarton Oaks Special Publication Series

Courtney, P, 2002, 'The pottery and tile', in Blockley and Halfpenney 2002, 93–98.

Cross, A, 1991, 'Russian gardens, British gardeners', *Garden History*, **19.1**, 12–20

Cruft, C H, 1991, 'The state of garden archaeology in Scotland', in Brown (ed) 1991, 175–89

Cunliffe, B, 1971 *Excavations at Fishbourne, 1961–69*, London: Res Rep Comm Soc Antiq

Currie, C K, 1988a, *Medieval fishponds: aspects of their origin, function, management and development*, MPhil thesis, University College, London

Currie, C K, 1988b, 'Medieval fishponds in Hampshire', in Aston (ed) 1988, ii, 267–89

Currie, C K, 1989, 'The role of fishponds in the monastic economy', Gilchrist, R, & Mytum, H (eds.), *The archaeology of rural monasteries*, BAR British series no **203**: Oxford: British Archaeological Reports, 147–72

Currie, C K, 1990a 'Southwick Priory fishponds: excavations 1987', *Proceedings of the Hampshire Field Club & Archaeological Society*, **46**, 53–72

Currie, C K, 1990b 'The excavation of an 18th-century garden pond: the West Pond, Castle Bromwich Hall, West Midlands', *Post-Medieval Archaeology* **24**, 93–123

Currie, C K, 1990c 'The role of environmental sampling in the interpretation of historic gardens', *West Midlands Archaeology*, **33**, 8–13

Currie, C. K, 1990d 'Fishponds as garden features, *c* 1550 – *c* 1750', *Garden History*, **18.1**, 22–46.

Currie, C K, 1992 'The restoration of historic gardens: the role of archaeology', *All natural things: archaeology and the green debate*, Macinnes, L, & Wickham-Jones, C (eds.), Oxford: Oxbow monograph **21**, 181–89

Currie, C K, 1993, "The archaeology of the flowerpot in England and Wales, 1650–1950", *Garden History* **21.2**, 227–46

Currie, C K, 1994a, *The Vyne estate, Sherborne St John, Hampshire: an archaeological survey*, unpublished client report

Currie, C K, 1994b, 'Historic wooden pipes found at Baddesley Clinton, Warwickshire', *Transactions of the Birmingham and Warwickshire Archaeological Society*, 98, 99–103

Currie, C K, 1995a 'Altered soils: a need for a radical revision of policy', pp 99–106, in Beavis, J, & Barker, K (eds.), *Science and site: evaluation and conservation* Poole: Bournemouth University School of Conservation Sciences

Currie, C K, 1995b 'Excavations in the park and gardens at Leigh Park, Havant, 1992', *Proceedings of the Hampshire Field Club and Archaeological Society*, **51**, 201–32

Currie, C K, 1995c 'Excavations in the gardens at The Wakes, Selborne, 1992', *Proceedings of the Hampshire Field Club and Archaeological Society*, **51**, 187–200

Currie, C K, 1995d, 'Horticultural wares from Ham House, Surrey', *Post-medieval archaeology*, **29**, 107–11

Currie, C K, 1996a 'Excavations in the gardens of Hanbury Hall, Worcestershire, 1991–3' *Transactions of the Worcestershire Archaeological Journal,* 3rd series, **15**, 225–44

Currie, C K, 1996b, 'Review of Thurley, S (ed), The King's Privy Garden at Hampton Court, 1689–1995', *Post-Medieval Archaeology*, **30**, 333–4

Currie, C K, 1997a, 'The boundaries of the medieval park at North Stoneham', *Hampshire Field Club and Archaeological Society Newsletter* new series no. **27**, 13–18

Currie, C K, 1997b, 'An archaeological assessment of a garden structure at Langton House, Milnthorpe Lane, Winchester, Hampshire', *Proceedings of the Hampshire Field Club & Archaeological Society*, **52**, 165–76

Currie, C K, 1998a, 'Earthworks in St Cross Park, near Winchester, Hampshire', *Proceedings of the Hampshire Field Club & Archaeological Society*, **53**, 169–82

Currie, C K, 1998b, 'The survival of historic garden features at Shaw House, near Newbury, Berkshire', *Transactions of the Newbury District Field Club*, **14.2/3**, 69–75

Currie, C K, 1998c, 'Clent Hills, Worcestershire: an archaeological and historical survey', *Transactions of the Worcestershire Archaeological Journal,* 3rd series, **16**, 183–206

Currie, C K, 2000a, 'Polesden Lacey and Ranmore Common estates, near Dorking, Surrey: an archaeological and historical survey', *Surrey Archaeological Collections*, **87**, 49–84

Currie, C K, 2000b, 'A watching brief on service trenches at Baddesley Clinton, Warwickshire', *Transactions of the Birmingham and Warwickshire Archaeological Society*, 102 (for 2000), 73–81

Currie, C K, 2001, 'The War Memorial (Goldings) Park, Basingstoke', *Hampshire Field Club and Archaeological Society Newsletter* new series no. **35**, 5–11

Currie, C K, 2003, 'Archaeological results at two Devon gardens, 1991–2000: Dartington Hall & Shilston Barton', in Wilson-North (ed) 2003**,** 50–63

Currie, C K, 2005, 'An archaeological survey of garden earthworks in Grotto Wood,

Roxford, Hertingfordbury, Hertfordshire', *Hertfordshire Archaeology*, **13**, (2005 for 1995–97)

Currie, C K, with Foster, P, & White, C, 2003 'Archaeological excavations at Upper Lodge, Bushy Park, London Borough of Richmond, 1997–1999', *Post-Medieval Archaeology*, **37.1**, 90–125

Currie, C K, & Locock, M, 1991a, 'An analysis of the archaeological techniques undertaken during the first year's excavations at Castle Bromwich Hall Gardens, 1989–90', *Garden History* **19.1**, 77–99

Currie, C K, & Locock, M, 1991b, *Oak House gardens, West Bromwich, West Midlands: an archaeological evaluation*, unpublished archive report deposited with Sandwell Metropolitan Borough Council

Currie, C K, & Locock, M, 1992 'Archaeology and the restoration of historic gardens: a maze of confusion', *The Field Archaeologist*, **17**, 332–34

Currie, C K, & Locock, M, 1993a 'Excavations at Castle Bromwich Hall gardens 1989–91' *Post-Medieval Archaeology*, **27**, 111–99

Currie, C K, & Locock, M, 1993b 'Trial excavations in the North Garden, Castle Bromwich Hall, West Midlands, 1991', *Transactions of the Birmingham and Warwickshire Archaeological Society*, **97**, 77–85

Currie, C K and Locock, M, 1995, The formal cascade at The Gnoll, *Welsh Historic Gardens Trust Newsletter* **8**, 72–79

Currie, C K, & Locock, M, 1997, 'The development of garden archaeology', *Institute of Field Archaeologists Yearbook and Directory of members 1997*, Manchester: Institute of Field Archaeologists, 23–25

Currie, C K, Locock, M, Howes, L, & O'Donovan, S, 1994 'Fishpond Wood Cascade, The Gnoll, West Glamorgan' *Archaeologia Cambrensis*, **163**, 236–71

Currie, C K & Rushton, N S, 2001, 'The historical development of Court of Noke, Pembridge, with an archaeological assessment of canal-like water features', *Transactions of the Woolhope Naturalists Field Club*, **50.2**, 224–50

Currie, C K, & Scholz, D, 1996 'Die Rolle der Archaologie in der Restaurierung historischer Garten', *Die Gartenkunst*, **8.1**, 161–70

Currie, C K, & Wade, S, 2003, *An archaeological and historical landscape survey of Priestlands School & its grounds, Lymington, Hants*, unpublished client report

Dalley, S, 1993, 'Ancient Mesopotamian gardens and the identification of the Hanging Gardens of Babylon resolved', *Garden History*, **21.1**, 1–13

David, P, 1999, *A Garden Lost in Time: The mystery of the ancient gardens of Aberglasney*, London: Weidenfeld and Nicolson

Department of the Environment 1990, *Planning Policy Guidance: archaeology and planning*, Planning Policy Guidance no 16, London: HMSO

Dickson, C, 1994, 'Macroscopic fossils of garden plants from British Roman and Medieval deposits', in Moe, D, Dickson, J H, & Jorgensen, P M (ed), *Garden history: garden plants, species, forms and varieties from Pompeii to 1800*, PACT, Rixensart, **42**, 47–72,

Dix, B, 1997, 'Digging of borders: reflections on archaeology and garden restoration', *Journal of Garden History*, **17.1**, 11–17

Dix, B, and Parry, S, 1995 'The excavation of the Privy Garden', in Thurley (ed), 1995, 79–118.

Dix, B, Soden, I, & Hylton, T 1995 'Kirby Hall and its gardens: excavations in 1987–1994' *Archaeological Journal*, **152**, 291–380

Elliott, B, 1986, *Victorian gardens*, London: Batsford

Emery, A, 1970, *Dartington Hall*, Oxford: Clarendon

English Heritage 2002, *Environmental archaeology. A guide to the theory and practice of methods, from sampling and recovery to post-excavation*, Portsmouth: Centre for Archaeology Guidelines

Everson, P, 1981 'Stallingborough earthwork survey', *Lincolnshire History and Archaeology*, **16**, 29–37.

Everson, P, 1989, 'The gardens of Campden House, Chipping Campden, Gloucestershire', *Garden History*, **17**.2, 109–121

Everson, P, 1991, 'Field survey & garden earthworks', Brown (ed) 1991, 6–19

Everson, P, 2003, 'Medieval gardens and designed landscapes', in Wilson-North (ed) 2003, 24–33

Ewart, G, 1990, *Excavation of the Orangery Garden at Tredegar House, 22–28 May 1990,* unpublished De Bois Landscape Group report to Newport City Council

Ewart, G and Phibbs, J, unpublished, *The Archaeological Excavation of Parts of the Orangery Garden, Tredegar House, Newport, Gwent, 1989–1991* (Kirkdale Archaeology report, copy in GGAT SMR)

Faegri, K & Iversen, J, 1975, *Textbook of pollen analysis*, Oxford: Blackwell Scientific, (2nd ed)

Farrar, R, 1987, *Survey by prismatic compass*, Practical handbooks in archaeology, no 2, London: CBA

Farrar, L, 1998, *Ancient Roman gardens*, Stroud: Sutton

Faulkner, P A, 1958, 'Domestic planning from the 12th to the 14th centuries', *Archaeological Journal*, **115**, 150–83

Ferguson, P F, 1999 'Indoor Gardening in the Eighteenth Century', *Antiques*, **CLV**.1, (January 1999), 168–177.

Festing, S 1984, 'Pulham has done his work well', *Garden History*, **12**.2, 138–58

Gaffney, C, Gater, J and Ovenden, S, 1991, *The Use of Geophysical Techniques in Archaeological Evaluations*, Institute of Field Archaeologists Technical paper **9**

Gallagher, C, 1996, 'The Leasowes: a history of the landscape', *Garden History*, **24**.2, 201–221

Gladwyn, D, 1992, *Leigh Park. A 19th century pleasure ground*, Midhurst: Middleton Press

Greig, J R A, 1971, 'Pollen analysis of the garden soil' in Cunliffe, B, 1971, *op cit*, 371–6

Green, A, & Bond, J, 1987, 'Blenheim after Vanbrugh: the second phase' in Bond, C J & Tiller, K (eds), *Blenheim: landscape for a palace*, Stroud: Sutton

Harvey, J, 1981, *Mediaeval gardens*, London: Batsford

Harvey, J, 1989, 'Garden plants of around 1525: the Fromond list', *Garden History*, **17**.2, 122–34

Harvey, J, 1992, 'Westminster Abbey: the infirmerer's garden', *Garden History*, **20**.2, 97–115

Hayden, P, (with comment by Currie, C. K.) 1993, 'Castle Bromwich Hall gardens: an alternative date', *Post-medieval archaeology* **27**, 201–04

Herring, P, 2003, 'Cornish medieval deer parks', in Wilson-North 2003, 34–50

Hicks, D, 2002, '"The garden of the world": a historical archaeology of East Caribbean Estates, 1600–present', unpublished PhD, University of Bristol

Hicks, D, 2005 forthcoming, 'Places for thinking from Annapolis to Bristol: Situations and symmetries' in 'World Historical Archaeology', *World Archaeology* **37**(3)

Higginbotham, J, 1997, *Piscinae: artificial fishponds in Roman Italy*, University of North Carolina Press: Chapel Hill

Hillier, B, & Hanson, J, 1985, *The social logic of space*, Cambridge: Cambridge University Press

Hogg, A H A 1980, *Surveying for archaeologists and other fieldworkers*, Croom Helm:

Hooper, W D 1934, *Res Rustica by Marcus Terrentius Varro*, London: Loeb Library

Howes, L 1991, 'Archaeology as an aid to restoration at Painshill Park', in Brown (ed) 1991, 73–82

Hughes, M.J, Cowell, M.R and Craddock, P.T. 1976. *Atomic absorption techniques in Archaeology*, Archaeometry, 18, 19–37.

Hume, A N, 1974, *Archaeology and the colonial gardener*, Colonial Williamsburg Archaeological Series no 7, Williamsburg, Virginia, USA

Hunt, J D & Willis, P, 1988, *The genius of the place: the English Landscape Garden 1620–1820*, London: MIT (revised edition)

Hussey, C, 1938, 'Dartington Hall part I', *Country Life*, 27th August 1938

Hussey, C, 1967, *English gardens and the landscape 1700–1750*, London: Country Life

Hutton, B, 1986 *Recording standing buildings*, Sheffield: Rescue

Hylton, T, 1995, 'Faunal remains', p 370, in Dix *et al* 1995

Hynd, N R, & Ewart, G, 1983 'Aberdour Castle Gardens', *Garden History*, **11.2**, 93–111

Inigo Triggs, H, 1989, *Formal gardens in England and Scotland*, Woodbridge: Antique Collectors' Club (1st ed, 1902 London: Batsford)

Jacques, D L, 1992, 'Garden archaeology and restoration', *Association for Studies in the Conservation of Historic Buildings Transactions*, **16**, 13–23

Johnson, M, 2002, *Behind the castle gate: from Medieval to Renaissance*, London: Routledge

Jones, F, 2002, 'Aberglasney and its families', in *The Francis Jones Treasury of Historic Carmarthenshire* (ed. C. Charles-Jones) (Newport, Pembrokeshire: Brawdy Books), 216–240; reprinted from *National Library of Wales Journal* **21** (1989).

Kenyon, J, 1993, 'Editorial', *Post-Medieval Archaeology*, **27**, vi

Land Use Consultants 1987, *An inventory of gardens and designed landscapes in Scotland*, Glasgow: Countryside Commission for Scotland

Landsberg, S, 1995, *The Medieval garden*, London: British Museum Press

Leathlean, H, 1995, 'From Gardenesque to Home Landscape: the garden journalism of Henry Noel Humphreys', *Garden History*, **23.2**, 175–91

Locock, M, 1990a for 1987–8 "18th century brickmaker's tally-marks from Castle Bromwich Hall", *Transactions of the Birmingham and Warwickshire Archaeological Society*, **95**, 95–8.

Locock, M, 1990b "The 18th century brickmaking industry in the Forest of Arden: Evidence from Castle Bromwich Hall", *Warwickshire History*, **8 (i)**, 3–20.

Locock, M, 1992 "The development of the building trades in the West Midlands, 1400–1850", *Construction History*, 8 (1992), 3–19.

Locock, M, 1993a 'Excavations in the walled garden, Bescot Hall, Walsall', *Transactions of the South Staffordshire Archaeological and Historical Society* **33**, 49–56

Locock, M 1993b, 'Metalwork', pp 182–83, in Currie, C K, & Locock, M, 1993a

Locock, M, 1993c, 'Glass', pp 180–81, in Currie, C K, & Locock, M, 1993a

Locock, M, 1993d, 'Brick and tile', pp 164–66, in Currie, C K, & Locock, M, 1993a

Locock, M, 1993e, 'Animal bone and shell', pp 185–87, in Currie, C K, & Locock, M, 1993a

Locock, M, 1994 'Spatial analysis of an 18th century formal garden', in Locock, M (ed.), *Meaningful architecture: social interpretations of buildings*, Worldwide Archaeology series no 9, Avebury: Ashgate Publishing, 231–52

Locock, M, 1995, 'The effectiveness of dowsing as a method of determining the nature and location of buried features on historic garden sites', *Archaeological Prospection* **2 i**, 15–18

Locock, M, 1998, Garden archaeology in South Wales, *Welsh Historic Gardens Trust Newsletter* (Spring 1998), 6–7

Locock, M, & Currie, C K, 1991 'Castle Bromwich Hall, excavations directed by P Twigg, 1985–8: a summary of the results', *West Midlands Archaeology*, **34**, 19–26

Locock, M with Currie, C K and Gray, S 1992 "Chemical changes in buried animal bone: data from a post-medieval assemblage", *International Journal of Osteoarchaeology*, **2**, 297–304.

Locock, M and Howell, J K, in press, 'Garden archaeology in southeast Wales: recent work', in Briggs, S (ed.), *Garden archaeology in Wales.*

Loudon, J C, 1838, *The suburban gardener and villa companion*, London

MacDougall, E B, & Jashemski, W F, 1981, *Ancient Roman gardens*, Dumbarton Oaks Colloquium no 7, Washington DC

Mackay, S, 2001, *Early Scottish gardens. A writer's odyssey*, Edinburgh: Polygon

Macphail, Crowther & Cruise 1995, 'The soils' in Thurley 1995, 116–18

Malek, A, & Conon, M, (eds) forthcoming *Handbook of Garden Archaeology*, Dumbarton Oaks, Washington DC

Marshall, G, 2002 'Threads of evidence: archaeology and the restoration of Stowe landscape gardens', *The National Trust. Annual archaeological review no 10, 2001–2002*, Cirencester: The National Trust, 19–23

McLean, T, 1981, *Medieval English gardens*, London: Collins

Melton, N, & Scott, K, 1999, 'Polesworth: A North Warwickshire country pottery', *Post-Medieval Archaeology*, **33**, 94–126

Moggridge, H, 1987, 'Capability Brown at Blenheim' in Bond, C J & Tiller, K (eds), *Blenheim: landscape for a palace*, Stroud: Sutton, 90–114

Moorhouse, S, 1991, 'Ceramics in the medieval garden', in Brown (ed) 1991, 100–17

Morris, M 1987, 'A possible icehouse at Milnethorpe [*sic*], Winchester', *Proceedings of the Hampshire Field Club & Archaeological Society*, **43**, 257–61

Morris, R, 1999, *Penllergare: A Victorian* paradise, Swansea: Penllergare Trust, Swansea

Murphy, K, in press, 'The Hafod landscape' in Briggs, S (ed.), *Garden archaeology in Wales.*

de Moulins, D, & Weir, D A, 1997, 'The potential and use of environmental techniques in gardens', *Journal of Garden History*, **17.1**, 40–46

Mowl, T, 1995, 'Rococo and later landscaping at Longleat', *Garden History*, **23.1**, 56–66

Murphy, P, & Scaife, R, 1991 'The environmental archaeology of gardens' in Brown (ed) 1991, 83–99

Nail, S, 1997, 'In pursuit of the authentic', *Historic Gardens Review*, **1**, 2–9

Neal, D S, Wardle, A and Hunn, J, 1990, *Excavation of the Iron Age, Roman and medieval settlement at Gorhambury, St Albans*, London: English Heritage Archaeological Report 14

Orton, C, 2000, *Sampling in archaeology*, Cambridge: Cambridge University Press

Palmer, R, & Cox, C, 1993, *Uses of aerial photography in archaeological evaluation*,

Technical Paper no 12, Birmingham: Institute of Field Archaeologists

Pearsall, D M, 1989, *Paleoethnobotany. A handbook of procedures*, New York: Academic Press

Phibbs, J, 1983 'An approach to the methodology of recording historic landscapes', *Garden History*, 11.2, 167–75

Phibbs, J, 1993, 'Pleasure grounds in Sweden and their English models', *Garden History*, **21.1**, 60–90

Platt, C, 1962, 'Excavations at Dartington Hall, 1962', *Archaeol. J.*, **119**, 208–24

Ponsford, M, 1992, 'Post-medieval Britain and Ireland in 1992', *Post-Medieval Archaeology*, **30**, 95–156

Ponsford, M, 2000, 'Post-medieval Britain and Ireland in 1998 and 1999', *Post-Medieval Archaeology*, **34**, 207–391

Ponsford, M, 2001, 'Post-medieval Britain and Ireland in 2000', *Post-Medieval Archaeology*, **37.2**, 122–289

Ponsford, M, 2003, 'Post-medieval Britain and Ireland in 2002', *Post-Medieval Archaeology*, **37.2**, 221–375

Ponsford, M, 2004, 'Post-medieval Britain and Ireland in 2003', *Post-Medieval Archaeology*, **38.2**, in press

Ponsford, M, forthcoming, 'Post-medieval Britain and Ireland in 2004', *Post-Medieval Archaeology*, **39.2**

Ponsford, M, & Jackson, R, 1996, 'Post-medieval Britain and Ireland in 1995', *Post-Medieval Archaeology*, **30**, 245–320

Ponsford, M & Jackson, R, 1997, 'Post-medieval Britain and Ireland in 1996', *Post-Medieval Archaeology*, **31**, 257–332

Rackham, O, 1986, *The history of the countryside*, London: Dent

RCHME, 1968 *West Cambridgeshire*, Inventory of historic monuments compiled by the Royal Commission on Historical Monument (England), London: HMSO

RCHME, 1972, *North-east Cambridgeshire*, Inventory of historic monuments compiled by the Royal Commission on Historical Monument (England), London: HMSO

RCHME 1975–82, *Northamptonshire I–IV*, Inventory of historic monuments compiled by the Royal Commission on Historical Monument (England), 4 vols., London: HMSO

Robertson, F W, 2000, *Early Scottish gardeners and their plants 1650–1750*, East Linton: Tuckwell

Rodwell, W J, and Rodwell, K A, 1986, *Rivenhall: investigations of a villa, church and village, 1950–1977*. CBA Research Report 55, London.

Roskams, S, 2001, *Excavation*, Cambridge: Cambridge University Press

de Rouffignac, C, 1995, 'Environmental sampling', in Currie 1995c, 228–31

de Rouffignac, C, & Currie, C K 1996, in Currie 1996a, 243

Samuels, A and Dixon Hunt, J , 1991, 'Aberglasney: "an enigmatic cloister range"', *Journal of Garden History* 11.3, 131–139

Sanecki, K, 1987, *Old garden tools*, Princes Risborough: Shire Books

Scaife, R 1995, 'Pollen analysis' in Thurley (ed) 1995, 116

Shackley, M, 1981, *Environmental archaeology*, London: George Allen & Unwin

Simo, M L, 1988, *Loudon and the landscape: from country seat to metropols, 1783–1843*, New Haven: Yale University Press

Singer, C, Holmyard, E J, Hall, A R, & Williams, T I (eds) 1958, *A history of technology*, vols IV & V, Oxford: Clarendon

Snell, R, 1989, *From the bare stem: making Dorothy Elmhirst's garden at Dartington Hall*, Exeter: Devon Books

Soden, I, 1995, *Excavations at St Anne's Charterhouse, Coventry 1986–87*, Coventry: Coventry Museums Monograph

Standing, D 2004, 'Some observations on the layout of Gilbert White's garden, Selborne: (1) The location of the Hercules statue', *Hampshire Field Club and Archaeological Society Newsletter, new series*, **41**, 11–13

Steane, J M 1977, 'The development of Tudor and Stuart garden design in Northamptonshire', *Northamptonshire Past and Present*, **5**, 383–406.

Strong, R, 1979, *The Renaissance garden in England*, London: Thames & Hudson

Stroud, D, 1962, *Humphry Repton*, London: Country Life

Stroud, D, 1975, *Capability Brown*, London: Faber & Faber

Switzer, S, 1729, *A universal system of water and water-works, philosophical and practical*, London

Symes, M, 1993, *A glossary of garden history*, Princes Risborough: Shire

Symes, M, 1996, *Garden sculpture*, Princes Risborough: Shire

Taigel, A, & Williamson, T, 1993, *Parks and gardens*, London: Batsford

Taylor, C C, 1983 *The archaeology of gardens*, Princes Risborough: Shire

Taylor, C C, 1988, 'Problems and possibilities' in Aston (ed) 1988, ii, 465–73

Taylor, C C, 1989, 'Somersham Palace, Cambridgeshire: a medieval landscape for pleasure?' in Bowden, M, Mackay, D, and Topping, P, (eds), *From Cornwall to Caithness*, BAR British series no **209**, Oxford: British Archaeological Reports, 211–24

Taylor, C C, 1998, *Parks and gardens of Britain: a landscape history from the air*, Edinburgh: Edinburgh University Press

Taylor, C C, 2000, 'Medieval Ornamental Landscapes', *Landscapes*, Macclesfield: Windgather

Taylor, C, Everson, P, & Wilson-North, R, 1990, 'Bodiam Castle, Sussex', *Medieval Archaeology*, **XXXIV**, 155–57

Taylor, H A, 1995, 'Urban public parks, 1840–199: design and meaning', *Garden History*, **23.2**, 201–21

Thurley, S, 1995, 'William III's Privy Garden at Hampton Court Palace: research and restoration', in Thurley, S (ed), *The King's Privy Garden at Hampton Court Palace, 1689–1995*, London: Apollo, 3–22

Turner, R C, 1992, Review of Brown, A E, (ed), 1991, 'Garden Archaeology', *Post-Medieval Archaeology*, **26**, 168–69

Van Leusen, M, 1999, 'Dowsing and archaeology: is there something underneath?', *Skeptical Inquirer*, March–April 1999.

Waterhouse, R, 2003, 'Garden archaeology in South Devon', in Wilson-North (ed) 2003, 66–82

Watkinson, D, (ed) 1987, *First aid for finds*, London: Rescue/United Kingdom Institute for Conservation

Whittle, E, 1989, 'The Renaissance gardens of Raglan Castle', *Garden History*, **17.1**, 83–94

Whittle, E, 1992, *The Historic Gardens of Wales: an introduction to parks and gardens in the history of Wales*, (Cadw: Welsh Historic Monuments), HMSO, London

Whittle, E, & Taylor, C, 1994, 'The early seventeenth-century gardens of Tackley,

Oxfordshire', *Garden History*, **22.1**, 37–63

Williams, R D, 1961, 'Llangathen and Aberglasney', *Carmarthenshire Antiquarian* **3**, 203–206.

Williamson, T, 1995, *Polite Landscapes. Gardens and society in eighteenth-century England*, Stroud: Sutton

Willis, P, 1978, *Charles Bridgeman and the English Landscape Garden*, London: Zwemmer

Wilson, D R, 1991, 'Old gardens from the air', in Brown (ed) 1991, 20–35

Wilson, D R, 2000, *Air photo interpretation for archaeologists*, Stroud: Sutton (revised ed, 1st ed 1982)

Wilson-North, R (ed), 2003, *The lie of the land. Aspects of the archaeology and history of the designed landscape in the South West of England*, Exeter: The Mint Press

Woodbridge, K, 1982, *The Stourhead landscape*, London: The National Trust

Woodfield, P, 1991, 'Early buildings in gardens in England' in Brown (ed) 1991, 123–37

Yentsch, A, & Kratzer, J M, 1997, 'Techniques used by historical archaeologists to study American landscapes and gardens', *Journal of Garden History*, **17.1**, 47–53

Yulle-Baddeley, D, 1994, Unpublished undergraduate thesis of garden soils, Department of Conservation Sciences, Bournemouth University

Zeepvat, R J, 1988, 'Fishponds in Roman Britain', in Aston, M (ed), 1988, *op cit*, 17–26

Zeepvat, R J, 1991, 'Roman gardens in Britain', in Brown, A E (ed), 1991, *op cit*, 53–59

The English *Register* and related matters

by Paul Stamper

To assist with the protection and long-term care of designed landscapes English Heritage is enabled, through the National Heritage Act 1983, to compile a register of gardens and other land in England considered by the organisation to be of special historic interest. The legislation is to be found in Section 8C of the Historic Buildings and Ancient Monuments Act 1953 (inserted by section 33 of, and paragraph 10 of Schedule 4 to, the National Heritage Act 1983). For the purpose of the *Register*, 'gardens and other land' is taken to embrace: gardens, parks, designed ornamental landscapes and places of recreation. 'Historic' is taken to embrace any site over 30 years old, the cut-off date rolling forward with the progress of time. As with listed buildings there is a I, II*, II grading system.

Inclusion of a site on the *Register* gives it a measure of protection, as Registration is 'a material consideration' in any planning application affecting such a site (*Planning Policy Guidance Note 15*, 2.24, September 1994). In such a case Local Planning Authorities are required to consult the Garden History Society (see below), and also English Heritage if the site is graded II* or I. Local authorities are also specifically guided towards protecting registered designed landscapes when preparing development plans (*PPG 15* 1.6, 2.4), and most now have policies intended to conserve not only registered sites but also those of more local interest.

The first edition of the *Register of Parks and Gardens of Special Historic Interest* was produced as a set of 46 county volumes, published between 1983 January 1988. Since then there has been a great increase in knowledge and interest historic designed landscapes, and this has been reflected in the sites included. Originally these were mainly landscape parks and gardens, but now also encompass town squares and walks, public parks, cemeteries, hospitals, allotments, pumping stations, sculpture gardens, civic spaces and college gardens.

Between 1996 and 2005 English Heritage carried out a comprehensive review and enhancement of the *Register* to upgrade and expand entries. In 2005 there were just under 1,600 registered sites. Copies of individual *Register* entries, and a booklet about the *Register*, can be obtained from the Enquiry and Research Services, National Monuments Record, Great Western Village, Kemble Drive, Swindon SN2 2GZ; tel. 01793 414 6000; fax 01793 414606; e mail inmrinfo@english-heritage.org.uk. From the late summer of 2005 it is anticipated that the Register will be available via the English Heritage website.

The Garden History Society, the amenity society for historic parks, gardens and designed landscapes, has conservation officers who comment on planning applications affecting registered sites and issues policy guidance. It has a programme of lectures and visits, and publishes the academic journal *Garden History*. It can be contacted at

70 Cowcross Street, London EC1M 6EJ;
tel. 0207 608 2409; fax 0207 490 2974;
e mail enquiries@gardenhistorysociety.org;
website www.gardenhistorysociety.org

Many counties now have gardens trusts, intended to foster an appreciation of their historic designed landscapes (see p 7). An umbrella organisation is The Association of County Gardens Trusts, also based at

70 Cowcross Street, London EC1M 6EJ;
tel. 0207 7251 2610; fax 0207 7251 2610;
e mail agt@gardens-trusts.org.uk;
website www.gardenstrusts.org.uk

For the planning system an essential guide is C Dingwall and D Lambert, *Historic Parks and Gardens in the Planning System: A Handbook* (Garden History Society/Landscape Design Trust, Reigate, 1997).

Index   *by Sue Vaughan*

Illustrations are denoted by page numbers in *italics*. The letter n following a page
number indicates that the reference will be found in a note.

171